The route to you

When they look back at their formative years, many Indians nostalgically recall the vital part Amar Chitra Katha picture books have played in their lives. It was **ACK – Amar Chitra Katha** – that first gave them a glimpse of their glorious heritage.

Since they were introduced in 1967, there are now **over 400 Amar Chitra Katha** titles to choose from. **Over 100 million copies** have been sold worldwide.

Now the Amar Chitra Katha titles are even more widely available in **1000+ bookstores all across India**. Log on to www.ack-media.com to locate a bookstore near you. If you do not have access to a bookstore, you can buy all the titles through our online store **www.amarchitrakatha.com**. We provide quick delivery anywhere in the world.

To make it easy for you to locate the titles of your choice from our treasure trove of titles, the books are now arranged in six categories.

Epics and Mythology
Best known stories from the Epics and the Puranas

Indian Classics
Enchanting tales from Indian literature

Fables and Humour
Evergreen folktales, legends and tales of wisdom and humour

Bravehearts
Stirring tales of brave men and women of India

Visionaries
Inspiring tales of thinkers, social reformers and nation builders

Contemporary Classics
The Best of Modern Indian literature

Amar Chitra Katha Pvt Ltd
© Amar Chitra Katha Pvt Ltd, 1972, Reprinted January 2017,
ISBN 978-81-8482-413-1
Published by Amar Chitra Katha Pvt. Ltd., 201 & 202, Sumer Plaza,
2nd Floor, Marol Maroshi Road, Andheri (East), Mumbai- 400 059. India
Printed at M/s Indigo press (I) Pvt Ltd., Mumbai.
For Consumer Complaints Contact Tel : +91-22 49188881/82/83
Email: customerservice@ack-media.com

The route to your roots

THE RANI
OF KITTUR

When Chenamma, the queen of Kittur, lost her only son she was steeped in sorrow. But when her husband reminded her that even the people of Kittur were her children she pulled herself together and devoted her life to their well-being. So committed was she to the honour and welfare of her land that when the British came asking for its allegiance she took on their military strength and fought them to the end.

Script	Illustrations	Editor
Rajalakshmi Raghavan	H.S.Chavan & Dilip Kadam	Anant Pai

THE RANI OF KITTUR

WHEN CHENNAMMA, THE DAUGHTER OF DHOOLAPPA GOWDA, THE DESAI *OF KAGATI, ꕔ MARRIED MALLASARJA, THE KING OF KITTUR; ꕔ SHE WAS BARELY SIXTEEN.

CHENNAMMA TOOK LEAVE OF HER FATHER WITH A HEAVY HEART.

CHENNA, SERVE YOUR HUSBAND, AND KITTUR WITH WHOLE-HEARTED DEVOTION.

WITH THE LOVING COUNSEL ECHOING IN HER HEART, CHENNAMMA LEFT FOR KITTUR.

* CHIEFTAIN   ꕔ NEAR BELGAUM IN KARNATAKA

ON THE WAY—

CHENNA, I AM OLDER THAN YOU BY SEVERAL YEARS. WERE YOU COAXED INTO ACCEPTING ME?

NO, INDEED, MY LORD! FOR ME IT WAS A DREAM FULFILLED.

A DREAM FULFILLED?

YES, MY LORD. WHEN I WAS NINE YEARS OLD MY FATHER TOLD ME HOW YOU TOILED IN TIPU'S* PRISON...

" ... HOW YOU BROKE OUT OF THE PRISON ...

* TIPU SULTAN OF MYSORE

"...AND HOW YOU WALKED OUT OF SRIRANGA PATTANA * DISGUISED AS A MENDICANT."

SINCE THEN I'VE BEEN WORSHIPPING YOU AS MY HERO.

WITH YOU BY MY SIDE, I WILL MAKE KITTUR STRONG AND SECURE.

WHEN THE PARTY REACHED THE PALACE, RANI RUDRAMMA, MALLASARJA'S FIRST WIFE, CAME OUT TO RECEIVE CHENNAMMA.

WELCOME, SISTER.

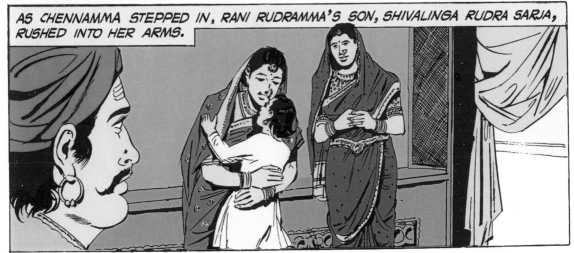

AS CHENNAMMA STEPPED IN, RANI RUDRAMMA'S SON, SHIVALINGA RUDRA SARJA, RUSHED INTO HER ARMS.

* TIPU'S CAPITAL

3

WHILE CHENNAMMA SOON WON THE AFFECTION OF ALL AT HER NEW HOME, THE PRINCE BECAME HER SPECIAL CHARGE.

TAKE THIS SWORD, SHIVA. I'LL TEACH YOU HOW TO WIELD IT.

RUDRAMMA AND MALLASARJA WERE TOUCHED AND PLEASED TO SEE THE INTEREST CHENNAMMA TOOK IN THE PRINCE.

SHE IS A BORN MOTHER.

LOOKING AT THEM, ONE WOULD BELIEVE THAT SHIVA WAS HER OWN SON.

A FEW YEARS LATER, CHENNAMMA TOO BORE A SON, BASAVARAJA, WHO GREW UP TO BE A BRAVE BOY.

WE'VE BEATEN MOTHER THIS TIME.

LET'S NOT BE FOOLED, BASAVARAJA. MOTHER HAS ALLOWED US TO OVERTAKE HER.

WHEN THEY CAME OF AGE, MALLASARJA ARRANGED THE WEDDING OF THE PRINCES. SHIVALINGA RUDRA SARJA MARRIED VEERAMMA AND BASAVARAJA, JANAKAMMA.

FIVE YEARS LATER, CHENNAMMA'S SON DIED.

CHENNA SITS BROODING ALL THE TIME. IT IS NOT GOOD FOR HER.

CHENNA, YOU WEEP FOR A SON WHO IS DEAD, WHILE THE REST OF YOUR CHILDREN REMAIN NEGLECTED.

CHENNAMMA WAS PERPLEXED.

THE REST OF MY CHILDREN—MY CHILDREN?

YES, CHENNA. AS THE QUEEN, ARE YOU NOT THE MOTHER OF ALL OUR SUBJECTS?

THE MESSAGE WENT HOME. CHENNAMMA WEPT NO MORE. SHE BEGAN TO TAKE A PERSONAL INTEREST IN THE WELFARE OF HER SUBJECTS.

RANI SAHEB, THE RAINS FAILED THIS YEAR, TOO. OUR VILLAGE FACES STARVATION.

DON'T WORRY. WE WILL HAVE GRAINS RUSHED TO YOUR VILLAGE.

SHE BEGAN TO TOUR EXTENSIVELY. ON ONE SUCH OCCASION —

WHO ARE YOU?

THE PORTUGUESE BROUGHT US AS SLAVES FROM AFRICA, RANI SAHEB. WE ESCAPED FROM GOA* BUT WE HAVE NO HOME.

MAKE KITTUR YOUR HOME. YOU SHALL BE GIVEN LAND.

RANI SAHEB, WE SHALL NEVER FORGET YOUR KINDNESS.

*GOA WAS THEN UNDER PORTUGUESE OCCUPATION

ON ANOTHER OCCASION—

YOUR MOSQUE IS IN RUINS. WHY DON'T YOU DO SOMETHING ABOUT IT?

AMATUR SAYID, A PIOUS MUSLIM STEPPED FORWARD.

WE WANT TO RENOVATE IT, RANI SAHEB. BUT WE DO NOT HAVE THE FUNDS.

HAVE IT RE-PAIRED. THE STATE WILL PAY FOR IT.

LATER, WHEN CHENNAMMA CAME TO SEE THE RENOVATED MOSQUE—

RANI SAHEB, IN YOU WE HAVE FOUND A MOTHER.

ONE DAY —

I HAVE BEEN SUMMONED BY THE PESHWA TO EDUR WHERE HE IS CAMP-ING. I'LL BE BACK SOON, CHENNA.

I HOPE THE PESHWA IS NOT ANNOYED WITH YOU FOR NOT CALLING ON HIM EARLIER.

A WEEK WENT BY BUT THERE WAS NO SIGN OF MALLASARJA.

WHAT COULD BE HOLDING HIM BACK? HE HASN'T SENT A MESSAGE EITHER.

SUSPECTING THAT MALLASARJA MIGHT ASSERT HIS INDEPENDENCE, THE PESHWA HAD CAPTURED HIM AT EDUR.

THE NEWS SOON REACHED CHENNAMMA.

RANI SAHEB, THE PESHWA HAS TAKEN THE KING PRISONER. HE IS AT PUNE.

CHENNAMMA SENT FOR GURU SIDDAPPA, A TRUSTED NOBLE.

GO TO PUNE, NEGOTIATE WITH THE PESHWA AND SECURE THE RELEASE OF THE KING.

I'LL START AT ONCE, YOUR MAJESTY.

MEANWHILE CHENNAMMA DID NOT ALLOW HER ANXIETY TO COME IN THE WAY OF HER ADMINISTRATION.

RANI CHENNAMMA IS AN EXCELLENT ADMINISTRATOR.

YES. I HAVE HARDLY FELT THE ABSENCE OF THE KING.

BUT WHEN SHE WAS ALONE IN THE PRIVACY OF HER CHAMBER—

WHEN WILL THE KING RETURN? IS HE ALL RIGHT? HAS GURU SIDDAPPA SUCCEEDED IN HIS MISSION?

FOR THREE ANXIOUS YEARS CHENNAMMA WAITED. THEN ONE DAY—

RANI SAHEB, I COME WITH GOOD NEWS! THE KING HAS BEEN SET FREE! HE IS ON HIS WAY TO KITTUR!

GOD BLESS YOU, MY SON. GOD BLESS YOU!

A FEW WEEKS LATER, GURU SIDDAPPA ARRIVED AT KITTUR.

WHERE IS THE KING? HAS HE SENT YOU IN ADVANCE TO INFORM US OF HIS RETURN? HOW IS HE?

HE FELL SERIOUSLY ILL IN PRISON. THAT WAS WHY HE WAS SET FREE.

I SHOULD HAVE BEEN INFORMED OF HIS ILLNESS. CAN HE STAND THE JOURNEY? WHERE IS HE NOW? WHEN WILL HE REACH KITTUR?

WHEN TOLD ABOUT IT, CHENNAMMA WAS SHOCKED.

SHIVA, ON NO ACCOUNT SHOULD YOU HELP THE ALIENS AGAINST OUR COUNTRY-MEN!

DON'T STOP ME, MOTHER! THE PESHWA KILLED MY FATHER. I WILL NOT LOSE THIS OPPORTUNITY TO AVENGE MY FATHER'S DEATH.

AND SHIVALINGA RUDRA SARJA SUMMONED MALLAPPA, HIS TRUSTED OFFICIAL.

INFORM THE BRITISH THAT THE FORCES OF KITTUR WILL FIGHT ON THEIR SIDE AT BELGAUM.

I WILL, YOUR MAJESTY. I'LL ALERT THE ARMY TOO.

AND DESPITE CHENNAMMA'S DISAPPROVAL, THE SOLDIERS OF KITTUR FOUGHT SIDE BY SIDE WITH THE BRITISH.

BELGAUM FELL. ACCOMPANIED BY MALLAPPA AND VENKATA RAO, SHIVALINGA RUDRA SARJA CALLED ON SIR THOMAS MUNRO.

WE RECOGNIZE YOU AND YOUR SUCCESSORS AS THE RULERS OF KITTUR. YOU WILL PAY US AN ANNUAL TRIBUTE OF A LAKH AND SEVENTY THOUSAND RUPEES.

WHEN SHIVALINGA RUDRA SARJA RETURNED TO KITTUR—

YOU HAVE STAINED THE HONOUR OF KITTUR BY SIGNING THAT TREATY!

BUT THE TREATY HAS BROUGHT US SECURITY. NOW WE HAVE THE PROTECTION OF THE BRITISH.

ALAS, MY SON!

LATER, A FRANTIC GURU SIDDAPPA CALLED ON CHENNAMMA.

RANI SAHEB, MALLAPPA AND VENKATA RAO ARE MISGUIDING THE KING. THEY ARE NOT TO BE TRUSTED. WHY DON'T YOU SPEAK TO THE KING?

I HAVE TRIED. HIS VALUES DIFFER FROM OURS. IT'S NO USE ADVISING HIM.

MEANWHILE SHIVALINGA RUDRA SARJA SUDDENLY FELL ILL.

MOTHER, I WON'T LIVE LONG. I HAVE NO SON. KITTUR NEEDS AN HEIR.

HUSH, MY SON. YOU'LL RECOVER.

BUT HIS CONDITION ONLY DETERIORATED. AT LAST ON HIS DEATH-BED, HE ADOPTED A SON.* AFTER THE CEREMONY—

MOTHER, WILL YOU TAKE CARE OF THE KINGDOM TILL MY SON COMES OF AGE?

I WILL, SHIVA.

GURU SIDDAPPA HURRIEDLY WROTE OUT A LETTER TO THE BRITISH, INFORMING THEM OF THE ADOPTION AND THE DYING KING SIGNED IT.

WHEN THE MESSAGE WAS DELIVERED THAT VERY DAY TO THACKERAY, THE BRITISH POLITICAL AGENT AT DHARWAR—

I WILL SEND DR. BELL TO KITTUR TO TREAT THE KING.

DR. BELL LEFT FOR KITTUR IMMEDIATELY.

*ON SUNDAY, SEPTEMBER 12, 1824

13

THE NEXT DAY, THACKERAY RECEIVED A LETTER FROM DR. BELL.

THE KING WAS DEAD BY THE TIME I REACHED KITTUR...

THACKERAY PICKED UP THE LETTER OF ADOPTION.

THE SIGNATURE OF THE KING DOESN'T LOOK GENUINE. IS IT A FORGED ONE? I'D BETTER VISIT KITTUR AND FIND OUT.

MEANWHILE AT KITTUR, THE UNTIMELY DEATH OF SHIVALINGA RUDRA HAD COME AS A BLOW TO MALLAPPA AND VENKATA RAO.

RANI CHENNAMMA IS THE OFFICIAL REGENT OF THE YOUNG KING! I AM WORRIED.

SO AM I. WE HAVE REASON TO BE. SHE DOESN'T TRUST US.

WE'LL HAVE TO GET RID OF HER BEFORE SHE GETS RID OF US.

HOW?

WE'LL SET THACKERAY AGAINST HER.

WHEN THACKERAY CAME TO KITTUR, THE TWO CONSPIRATORS CALLED ON HIM.

YOU'VE COME AT THE RIGHT TIME, SIR. THERE IS ANARCHY BREWING IN THE STATE.

THE KING IS BUT A LITTLE BOY; THE REGENT A WOMAN.

THE PURPOSE OF MY VISIT IS TO STUDY THE SITUATION HERE. TELL ME, MALLAPPA, WHEN DID THE KING DIE?

ON SATURDAY... EVENING... NO... NO... IT WAS SUNDAY!

ENOUGH! YOU MAY GO NOW.

AS THE TWO CONSPIRATORS RETURNED TO THE FORT—

THAT WAS PERFECT, MALLAPPA. THE TONE... THE MANNER ... AS IF THE TRUTH HAD SLIPPED OUT...

NOW THACKERAY WILL SUSPECT FOUL PLAY AND WILL REFUSE TO RECOGNIZE THE ADOPTION.

LATER, WHEN GURU SIDDAPPA CALLED ON THACKERAY—

DON'T YOU KNOW THAT WE DO NOT RECOGNIZE AN ADOPTION UNLESS OUR PRIOR APPROVAL IS TAKEN?

THERE WAS NO TIME, SIR. THE KING WAS ON HIS DEATH-BED AND...

AND HE DIED BY THE TIME YOU GOT THE LETTER OF ADOPTION READY!

WHAT DO YOU MEAN, SIR?

YOU KNOW WHAT I MEAN. THE PEN WITH WHICH ONE OF YOU SIGNED WAS THRUST INTO THE LIFELESS HAND OF THE DEAD DESAI.

THIS IS AN AFFRONT! TAKE BACK YOUR WORDS, SIR.

THACKERAY REMAINED ADAMANT.

I'LL SEND MY REPORT TO MR.CHAPLIN.MEANWHILE, I WANT LAW AND ORDER TO BE MAINTAINED IN KITTUR.

WE HAVE NEVER NEEDED YOUR HELP FOR THAT AND WE DON'T NEED IT NOW!

WHEN GURU SIDDAPPA REPORTED THE TALK HE HAD WITH THACKERAY TO THE QUEEN—

WE WILL NOT TOLERATE THE HIGH-HANDED BEHAVIOUR OF THE ENGLISH COLLECTOR! LET THE COUNCILLORS MEET TO DISCUSS THE ISSUES RAISED BY HIM.

MEANWHILE THACKERAY HAD ENTERED THE FORT WITH HIS MEN...

...AND MARCHED INTO THE TREASURY.

THE TREASURY SHALL BE SEALED! NO MONEY SHALL BE DRAWN WITHOUT MY PERMISSION.

LATER, POSTING HIS OWN GUARDS THERE, HE RETURNED TO HIS CAMP.

THE COUNCILLORS WERE FURIOUS.

THIS IS AN OUTRAGE!

ARE WE TO TAKE IT LYING DOWN?

LET'S WAIT AND SEE WHAT RANI SAHEB HAS TO SAY ABOUT IT.

RANI CHENNAMMA SOON HAD MUCH TO SAY.

SHOULD WE ALLOW OUTSIDERS TO INTERFERE IN OUR AFFAIRS?

NO!

NO!

TODAY WE ARE ASKED TO BEND. TOMORROW WE MAY HAVE TO CRAWL. WE SHOULD FIGHT FOR OUR RIGHTS.

RANI SAHEB, JUSTICE IS ON OUR SIDE BUT··· TIPU SULTAN FELL FIGHTING THE BRITISH··· AND THE PESHWA HAS BEEN VANQUISHED BY THEM.

RANI CHENNAMMA SPOKE SOFTLY BUT FIRMLY.

I AM NOT EAGER TO PLUNGE INTO A WAR WITH THE BRITISH. I'LL TRY FOR A PEACEFUL SETTLEMENT; I'LL WRITE TO CHAPLIN.* BUT IF WE HAVE TO FIGHT, FIGHT WE MUST.

MEANWHILE, PEOPLE IN THE VILLAGES CAME TO KNOW OF THE THREAT TO THE STATE.

ARROGANT THACKERAY IS THREATENING OUR PIOUS QUEEN. LET'S RUSH TO HER HELP.

YOU ARE RIGHT, RAYANNA. LET US START WITHOUT DELAY.

✳ THE DECCAN COMMISSIONER AT PUNE

LOYAL SUBJECTS BEGAN TO POUR INTO KITTUR FORT FROM FAR AND NEAR.

WE WILL NOT PERMIT THE ALIENS TO HARASS OUR RANI SAHEB.

WE'LL THROW THEM OUT OF KITTUR.

CHENNAMMA WAS MOVED BY THE WHOLE-HEARTED DEVOTION AND LOYALTY OF HER SUBJECTS.

I AM GRATEFUL TO YOU FOR YOUR SUPPORT. I NEED IT. I REQUEST YOU TO BE CALM. I WANT TO AVOID BLOODSHED IF I CAN.

MEANWHILE AT THACKERAY'S CAMP—

SIR, THE FORT IS SWELLING WITH ARMED MEN. I EXPECT TROUBLE.

I WILL MEET RANI CHENNAMMA. FIND OUT WHEN IT WILL BE CONVENIENT FOR HER.

AFTER SOME TIME THE OFFICER RETURNED.

RANI CHENNAMMA HAS DECLINED TO MEET YOU, SIR. SHE SAID IT WILL SERVE NO USEFUL PURPOSE.

THE NEXT DAY—

SIR, THEY HAVE CLOSED THE GATE OF THE FORT AND NO COUNCILLOR IS PREPARED TO MEET US.

THEN LET'S MARCH TO THE FORT.

BUT WHEN THACKERAY RODE UP TO THE FORT WITH HIS MEN—

SIR, THEY REFUSE TO OPEN THE GATE, IN SPITE OF REPEATED WARNINGS.

CAPTAIN BLACK, GET YOUR CANNONS HERE. IF THEY WON'T RESPOND TO OUR POLITE REQUESTS, WE'LL COERCE THEM. IF THEY DON'T OPEN THE GATE, WE'LL BLAST IT OPEN.

THE CANNONS WERE STATIONED IN FRONT OF THE GATE. THACKERAY ISSUED THE FINAL WARNING.

WE'LL GIVE YOU TWENTY-FOUR MINUTES. IF THE GATE IS NOT OPENED BY THEN, WE'LL LAUNCH A CANNONADE.

AT THE PALACE—

RANI SAHEB, THE ARMY IS READY. WE ARE AWAITING YOUR ORDER.

THEY LEAVE US NO CHOICE. CHAPLIN HAS NOT RESPONDED TO OUR PLEAS. THACKERAY IS ADAMANT. THE WAR IS FORCED UPON US. AND YET...

CHENNAMMA WAVERED.

CAN A SMALL KINGDOM FIGHT A MIGHTY EMPIRE?

THEN SHE HAD A STRANGE VISION.

FIGHT, CHENNA. UPHOLD THE HONOUR OF KITTUR. FIGHT, MY DEAR.

TIME IS RUNNING OUT, RANI SAHEB!

I AM READY, GURU SIDDAPPA. I'LL PERSONALLY ANNOUNCE MY DECISION TO THE PEOPLE.

MEANWHILE THE SOLDIERS OF KITTUR WERE GETTING RESTLESS.

WHY DOES RANI SAHEB HESITATE?

TO THEIR UTTER SURPRISE, THE RANI APPEARED BEFORE THEM, FULLY ARMED AND RIDING A HORSE.

MY BRAVE MEN, WE WILL FIGHT TO SHOW THE WORLD THAT PEOPLE OF EVEN A SMALL STATE LIKE OURS VALUE HONOUR AND INDEPENDENCE ABOVE EVERYTHING ELSE. FIGHT WE WILL!

HAIL RANI CHENNAMMA!

GURU SIDDAPPA RUSHED TOWARDS HER.

RANI SAHEB, PLEASE GO BACK TO THE PALACE. LEAVE US TO DO THE FIGHTING.

I HAVE DECIDED TO LEAD MY MEN.

MEANWHILE THACKERAY'S MEN WERE WAITING PATIENTLY.

THEY WILL OPEN THE GATE.

SEE WHAT DID I SAY?

WE HAVE WON— WITHOUT A SHOT BEING FIRED!

BUT TO THEIR GREAT SURPRISE, CHENNAMMA'S SOLDIERS POURED OUT OF THE FORT SHOUTING WAR CRIES.

RANI CHENNAMMA KI JAI!

HAR HAR MAHDEV*!

*A WAR CRY

WHEN SAYID BALAPPA, A MUSLIM BODYGUARD OF CHENNAMMA TOOK AIM AT THACKERAY —

NO, BALAPPA! NOT HIM!

BUT BALAPPA HAD ALREADY PRESSED THE TRIGGER.

AS THACKERAY FELL, GURU SIDDAPPA, RAYANNA AND OTHER VETERANS SWOOPED DOWN ON THE RETREATING ENEMY...

...AND SEVERAL OF THEM WERE TAKEN PRISONERS.

FOR THE CHEERING CROWD, CHENNAMMA HAD A WORD OF CAUTION.

NOW WE ARE COMMITTED TO THE PATH OF CONFRONTATION WITH THE BRITISH. THIS VICTORY OF OURS IS NOT THE DECISIVE ONE. WE MUST BE VIGILANT.

THE VICTORY OF RANI CHENNAMMA CAME AS A BLOW TO THE BRITISH. CHAPLIN, THE DECCAN COMMISSIONER RUSHED FROM PUNE TO BELGAUM AND HELD TALKS WITH THE COMMANDING OFFICERS.

A WOMAN HAS HUMBLED OUR PRIDE. SHE MUST BE CRUSHED.

YES, SIR. IF KITTUR GOES UNPUNISHED THE OTHER INDIAN STATES ALSO MAY REBEL.

RALLY OUR FORCES AND CAPTURE KITTUR.

THE BRITISH FORCES FROM BOMBAY AND MADRAS ARRIVED AT KITTUR AND LAID SIEGE TO THE FORT.

OUR TASK WOULD HAVE BEEN MUCH EASIER IF MALLAPPA AND VENKATA RAO WERE ALIVE. THE RANI FOUND OUT THEIR TREACHERY AND HAD THEM PUT TO DEATH.

WHAT IF THEY ARE DEAD? THERE MUST BE MANY SUCH.

CHAPLIN WAS NOT YET READY TO FIRE THE FIRST SHOT.

I'LL STALL FOR TIME TILL PEARS JOINS ME WITH HIS BATTERING TRAIN. NO HARM IN CARRYING ON NEGOTIATIONS WITH THE RANI TILL THEN.

AS THE BATTERING TRAIN RUMBLED THROUGH THE MARSHY TRACK FROM BELGAUM TO KITTUR···

···CHAPLIN NEGOTIATED WITH CHENNAMMA'S ENVOY.

THE RANI MUST FIRST SET HER ENGLISH PRISONERS FREE. ONLY THEN CAN THERE BE ANY TALK OF PEACE.

BRIEFED BY RANI CHENNAMMA, THE ENVOY CALLED ON CHAPLIN AGAIN.

OUR RANI IS PREPARED TO RELEASE THE BRITISH PRISONERS, IF YOU ASSURE US THAT YOU WILL RAISE THE SIEGE.

WE WILL, IF THE RANI AND ALL HER COUNCILLORS SURRENDER.

WHEN THE ENVOYS REPORTED CHAPLIN'S CONDITIONS TO CHENNAMMA —

NEVER SHALL I SURRENDER! I KNOW I'LL BE FIGHTING A LOSING BATTLE. YET FIGHT I MUST TO REDEEM THE HONOUR OF KITTUR.

AS SOON AS THE BATTERY TRAIN ARRIVED, CHAPLIN ISSUED A FINAL WARNING.

IF THE PRISONERS ARE NOT RELEASED AND THE FORT IS NOT SURRENDERED BEFORE TEN TOMORROW MORNING, THE FIRING WILL BEGIN···

CHENNAMMA CALLED GURU SIDDAPPA.

RELEASE THE PRISONERS.

RANI SAHEB, WE ARE SAFE AS LONG AS WE HOLD THEM. IF WE RELEASE THEM, THE BRITISH WILL MERCILESSLY ATTACK US.

I REALISE THAT. I DON'T WANT TO TAKE COVER BEHIND THE BRITISH PRISONERS. RELEASE THEM AND ASK OUR MEN TO BE PREPARED TO FIGHT TO A FINISH.

THE PRISONERS WALKED OUT OF THE FORT. TWO OF THEM, STEVENSON AND ELIOT CALLED ON CHAPLIN.

SIR, WE WERE TREATED WELL BY THE RANI. SHE WANTS FRIENDSHIP WITH THE BRITISH. AVOID BLOODSHED, SIR.

IT IS TOO LATE NOW, TO TALK OF PEACE.

AS THE BRITISH TROOPS ADVANCED, CHENNAMMA'S MEN OPENED FIRE.

THE BRITISH CANNONS KEPT FIRING INCES-SANTLY AND THE NEXT DAY A PORTION OF THE FORT WAS BLOWN UP.

THE ENEMY POURED INTO THE FORT AND A FIERCE BATTLE FOLLOWED.

CHENNAMMA LOST HEAVILY AND WAS FINALLY TAKEN PRISONER.

MY ONLY REGRET IS THAT I COULDN'T DIE FIGHTING ON THE BATTLEFIELD.

BEFORE SHE LEFT KITTUR, SHE TOOK ONE LAST LOOK AT HER FORT.

THE BRITISH FLAG ATOP OUR FORT! I WILL KNOW PEACE ONLY WHEN THE SHACKLE OF SLAVERY IS BROKEN. GOD HELP KITTUR, HELP MY COUNTRY!

CHENNAMMA WAS TAKEN TO BAILAHONGALA FORT WHERE FIVE YEARS LATER, SHE DIED. EVEN TO THIS DAY THE PEOPLE OF KITTUR SING ABOUT THEIR VALOROUS QUEEN WHO WAS AMONG THE FIRST TO RESIST THE BRITISH RULE IN INDIA— A FORERUNNER OF THE RANI OF JHANSI.

RANI OF JHANSI

THE FLAME OF FREEDOM

The route to your roots

RANI OF JHANSI

She ruled over a small kingdom, but dreamt of freedom for the whole country. In the Great Revolt of 1857, Lakshmibai, the Rani of Jhansi, matched wits and force with the best of British generals. The image of the brave Rani of Jhansi charging her steed through enemy lines, her sword raised for the next thrust, is forever imprinted in Indian hearts.

Script	Illustrations	Editor
Mala Singh	Hema Joshi	Anant Pai

Cover illustration by: Pratap Mulick

RANI OF JHANSI

THE EXILED PESHWA, BAJIRAO II LIVED AT BITHUR, WITH HIS FAMILY. ONE OF HIS COURTIERS, MOROPANT HAD A DAUGHTER NAMED MANIKARNIKA.

MANU, AS HER PLAYMATES CALLED HER, LOVED TO READ AND WRITE.

HAVE YOU SEEN MANU?

SHE'S STUDYING WITH THE BOYS.

FOR WHAT? LEARNING IS OF LITTLE USE TO A WOMAN!

BUT MANU IS DESTINED TO BE A QUEEN!

THE YEARS PASSED AND WHEN MANU WAS ELEVEN YEARS OLD—

MANU IS GETTING OLD! ISN'T IT TIME YOU FOUND A HUSBAND FOR HER?

THE ASTROLOGERS HAVE FORETOLD A ROYAL MATCH FOR HER!

HAVE YOU HEARD THE NEWS? OUR MANU IS TO MARRY THE MAHARAJA OF JHANSI!

AND SHE WILL BE NAMED LAKSHMIBAI, IN HONOUR OF THE GODDESS OF WEALTH AND VICTORY!

AND SO ANOTHER YEAR PASSED.

THE WEDDING WAS CELEBRATED WITH GREAT POMP...

...AND CEREMONY IN MAY 1842.

IN 1851 LAKSHMIBAI GAVE BIRTH TO A SON.

THIS IS A HAPPY DAY FOR JHANSI!

BUT THREE MONTHS LATER THE CHILD DIED.

THE MAHARAJA WAS PLUNGED IN GRIEF AND DESPAIR.

ALAS! I HAVE NO SON TO SUCCEED ME! WHAT SHALL I DO?

THE MAHARAJA IS DYING!

WHAT WILL HAPPEN TO JHANSI?

THE MAHARAJA HAS DECIDED TO ADOPT A SON!

THE ADOPTION TOOK PLACE ON NOVEMBER 19, 1853.

A DAY LATER THE MAHARAJA DIED.

THE FATE OF THE PEOPLE OF JHANSI IS NOW IN MY HANDS! I MUSTN'T LET THEM DOWN!

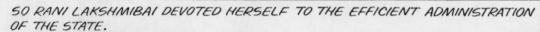

SO RANI LAKSHMIBAI DEVOTED HERSELF TO THE EFFICIENT ADMINISTRATION OF THE STATE.

THIS MAN SAYS, YOU HAVE USURPED HIS LAND. WHAT HAVE YOU TO SAY IN YOUR DEFENCE?

THERE WAS A DROUGHT LAST YEAR. I'LL LOWER THE TAX ON WHEAT.

LAKSHMIBAI SENT A PETITION TO THE GOVERNOR GENERAL FOR THE RECOGNITION OF HER ADOPTED SON.

BUT THE GOVERNOR GENERAL REJECTED THE PETITION.

THE BRITISH GOVERNMENT HAS DECIDED TO TAKE THE STATE OF JHANSI UNDER ITS WING.

I WILL NOT GIVE UP MY JHANSI!

IT WAS A DAY OF MOURNING, IN JHANSI.

THE COMPLETE SUPPORT OF HER PEOPLE RENEWED LAKSHMIBAI'S SPIRIT.

THE RANI OF JHANSI WAS NOT BORN TO WEEP! I WILL SEND AN ENVOY TO LONDON WITH AN APPEAL.

BUT—

THE BRITISH HAVE REJECTED YOUR APPEAL!

THEY HAVE NO SENSE OF JUSTICE. I WILL NOT OBEY THEM.

THE BRITISH WERE BECOMING MORE AND MORE UNPOPULAR.

THEY ANNEXED SATARA WITHOUT JUSTI- FICATION.

OUR ANCIENT HANDLOOM INDUSTRY HAS BEEN RUINED BY CHEAP BRITISH CLOTH.

ON MAY 10, 1857 THE GARRISON OF MEERUT OPENLY REVOLTED, SHOT THEIR OFFICERS AND RELEASED IMPRISONED COMRADES.

THEN THEY MARCHED TO DELHI WHERE THEY RECEIVED A WARM WELCOME.

THE AGED EX-EMPEROR WAS REINSTATED ON THE MUGHAL THRONE AND DELHI BECAME THE HEADQUARTERS OF THE NATIONALIST SOLDIERS.

9

THE BRITISH RAN TO LAKSHMIBAI AND BEGGED FOR HELP.

WE WANT YOU TO TAKE OVER THE KINGDOM UNTIL BRITISH AUTHORITY IS RE-ESTABLISHED.

YOU REFUSED ME MY KINGDOM WHEN I ASKED FOR IT. NOW THAT YOU CANNOT KEEP IT, YOU ARE HANDING IT TO ME! THE INDIAN TROOPS WILL DESTROY ME IF I GIVE YOU PROTECTION. YOU HAD BETTER SAVE YOUR LIVES AS BEST YOU CAN.

THE BRITISH WERE POWERLESS AGAINST THE NATIONALIST SOLDIERS AND WERE COMPLETELY ROUTED.

LET'S GO TO DELHI AND LEAVE LAKSHMIBAI TO RULE JHANSI.

THE POOR RANI HAS ALSO BEEN TREATED BADLY BY THE BRITISH!

BUT RANI LAKSHMIBAI CALLED A CONFERENCE OF ALL CLASSES OF HER PEOPLE.

I WANT MY PEOPLE TO DECIDE WHO SHOULD RULE JHANSI!

FOR THE TIME BEING, RANI SAHIBA SHOULD ASSUME CONTROL.

THE RANI WILL RULE JHANSI FOREVER!

WE ARE LOYAL SUBJECTS OF THE RANI OF JHANSI!

A LARGE CROWD WAS ANXIOUSLY WAITING OUTSIDE FOR THE DECISION OF THEIR REPRE-SENTATIVES.

LAKSHMIBAI WILL RULE AND JHANSI WILL BE INDEPENDENT!

LONG LIVE LAKSHMIBAI!

VICTORY TO OUR RANI!

WE HAVE COME TO PERFORM RAMLEELA.

WELCOME! THE RANI WILL BE PLEASED TO SEE YOU!

LAKSHMIBAI WAS A GREAT PATRONESS OF ART AND LITERATURE.

THE STATE LIBRARY WAS LAKSHMIBAI'S SPECIAL INTEREST. SHE OFTEN BOUGHT NEW BOOKS REGARDLESS OF THEIR COST.

THE FIRST CHALLENGE TO LAKSHMIBAI'S RULE CAME FROM SADASHIV RAO, A DISTANT NEPHEW OF THE LATE MAHARAJA.

I AM THE KING OF JHANSI.

THE RANI OF JHANSI IS OUR RULER.

LAKSHMIBAI SENT HER TROOPS AGAINST HIM AND DEFEATED HIM IN A SINGLE ENCOUNTER.

THE PRINCES OF DATIA AND ORCHA, TWO NEIGHBOUR STATES, TRIED TO WREST JHANSI FROM LAKSHMIBAI BUT HER TROOPS DEFEATED THEM.

THE SOLDIERS OF ORCHA ARE APPROACHING!

LET THEM DO THEIR UTMOST! WE WILL NOT GIVE UP JHANSI!

WE MUST NOT WASTE MEN NEEDLESSLY. WE'LL ONLY ATTACK WHEN THEY ARE NEAR.

THE JHANSI SOLDIERS ARE NOT FIRING! LET'S GO FORWARD AND TAKE THE FORT!

LAKSHMIBAI'S TROOPS OPENED FIRE AND THE INVADERS RETREATED IN CONFUSION.

BOOM!

BOOM!

THE ORCHA TROOPS SILENTLY MOVED FOUR GUNS UNDER THE COVER OF DARKNESS AND MADE A MASSIVE ATTACK ON THE JHANSI FORCES.

WE ARE DEFEATED! ALL IS LOST.

DON'T LOSE COURAGE! JHANSI NEVER ADMITS DEFEAT!

ENCOURAGED BY THEIR QUEEN, THE JHANSI TROOPS ROUTED THE ENEMY.

RANI LAKSHMIBAI HELD A GRAND DURBAR TO CELEBRATE HER VICTORY.

I AM PROUD OF MY MEN! YOU ARE BRAVE AND FEARLESS!

HOWEVER THERE WAS BAD NEWS FROM DELHI.

THE BRITISH HAVE CAPTURED DELHI!

WHAT'S HAPPENED TO THE EMPEROR?

HIS SONS WERE TREACHEROUSLY SHOT. THE EMPEROR HAS BEEN IMPRISONED.

NANA SAHEB'S ARMY HAS BEEN DEFEATED AND KANPUR REOCCUPIED.

ALL OF OUDH HAS BEEN RECONQUERED BY THE BRITISH.

WILL IT BE JHANSI'S TURN NEXT?

SO LAKSHMIBAI BEGAN TO MAKE PREPARATIONS TO FACE AN ATTACK FROM THE BRITISH.

WE MUST HAVE A FIRE-BRIGADE!

WE WILL HAVE TO PROCURE MORE ARMS.

ARE THERE ENOUGH STORES OF FOOD AND FODDER TO MEET A LONG SIEGE?

THEN THE RANI CALLED FOR MEN TO ENLIST IN HER ARMY.

I WILL!

HOW MANY OF YOU WILL FIGHT FOR YOUR JHANSI?

WE ALL WILL!

THE WOMEN OF JHANSI, TOO, MUST HELP!

WHAT CAN WE DO?

WOMEN WERE ENLISTED AS TROOPERS AND GUNNERS AND TAUGHT TO RIDE, SHOOT AND FENCE. THEY TOOK ON WATCH DUTIES AND CARED FOR THE WOUNDED.

LAKSHMIBAI HELD A HALDI-KUMKUM CEREMONY TO INSPIRE CONFIDENCE IN THE WOMEN.

THE BRITISH HAVE CAPTURED SEHORE AND RAHATGARH!

THEY HAVE TAKEN SAGAR!

THEY'VE DEFEATED OUR ALLY, THE RAJA OF BANPUR!

THEY'LL BE AT OUR GATES WITHIN A FEW WEEKS!

MEANWHILE, IN THE BRITISH CAMP—

DON'T UNDERESTIMATE THE RANI OF JHANSI! SHE'S THE BEST ONE ON THE REBEL SIDE!

NOW THAT THE FORT OF CHANDERI IS IN OUR HANDS, JHANSI IS ALMOST OURS!

WHY DON'T YOU ASK YOUR OLD FRIENDS TATYA TOPE AND RAO SAHEB FOR HELP?

I HAVE. TATYA TOPE HAS ALREADY ATTACKED THE RAJAS OF PANNA AND CHARKHARI, STAUNCH ALLIES OF THE BRITISH.

HE CAPTURED 24 GUNS AND TOOK RS. 3,00,000!

BUT THE BRITISH ARE STILL DETERMINED TO ATTACK JHANSI!

LAKSHMIBAI CALLED A REPRESENTATIVE MEETING OF HER PEOPLE AND ASKED IF THEY WANTED TO DEFEND THE CITY OR SUE FOR PEACE.

I THINK WE SHOULD FIGHT BUT I LEAVE THE DECISION IN YOUR HANDS!

WE SHOULD SAVE OUR HOMES. I'M AGAINST WAR.

NO, WE'LL FIGHT! WE'LL UPHOLD THE INDEPENDENCE OF JHANSI!

NO FOREIGNER WILL RULE JHANSI!

YES!

LONG LIVE LAKSHMI-BAI!

YOU HAVE TAKEN A BRAVE AND NOBLE DECISION. WE'LL FIGHT! IF VICTORIOUS WE'LL ENJOY FREEDOM. IF DEFEATED OR SLAIN WE EARN ETERNAL GLORY!

VICTORY TO OUR QUEEN!

EARLY ON MARCH 25, 1858 BRITISH GUNS BEGAN TO BOMBARD JHANSI. BUT LAKSHMIBAI'S GUNNERS ANSWERED SHOT FOR SHOT.

BOOM!

BANG!

BOOM!

BOOM!

FOR 5 DAYS THE BRITISH GUNS POUNDED DAY AND NIGHT BUT WITH LITTLE RESULT.

THEN A PARAPET AND TOWER WERE SLIGHTLY DAMAGED.

COME ON, LET'S REPAIR THE BREACH!

WE'LL NEVER LET THE FOREIGNER IN!

LOOK! TATYA TOPE IS COMING TO OUR RESCUE!

WE'RE SAVED!

IT'S TATYA TOPE.

THEY'VE LIT AN ENORMOUS BONFIRE!

THE BRITISH WILL NEVER RULE JHANSI.

AT NIGHT THE BRITISH BROUGHT TWO 24-POUNDERS AND BOMBARDED TATYA'S MEN.

AND THE NEXT DAY THE BRITISH ROUTED TATYA'S ARMY IN A SINGLE ENCOUNTER.

LAKSHMIBAI ASSEMBLED HER OFFICERS.

ALL IS LOST!

WE MUSTN'T LOSE HEART. WE CAN FIGHT THE BRITISH ALONE. YOU HAVE FOUGHT WITH MATCH-LESS COURAGE BEFORE. I AM DEPENDING ON YOU. I KNOW YOU WILL DO IT!

WE WILL FIGHT TO THE LAST MAN.

VICTORY WILL BE OURS!

WE WON'T GIVE UP.

21

ON APRIL 3, 1858 —

LOOK! THERE'S WHERE WE SHOULD CLIMB!

OUR ALLY IN THE QUEEN'S CAMP HAS KEPT HIS WORD!

HE WAS WELL-PAID!

THE BRITISH ARE UPON US!

LET THEM COME! WE'LL SHOW THEM HOW THE MEN OF JHANSI FIGHT!

THE BRITISH ARE INSIDE THE FORT.

THERE'S NO HOPE NOW! ALL CHANCE OF VICTORY IS LOST! SHOULD I SURRENDER?

NO, NEVER!

AND LAKSHMIBAI AT THE FOREFRONT OF HER TROOPS CHARGED AT THE BRITISH.

THE COUNTER ATTACK WAS SO UNEXPECTED AND FIERCE THAT THE BRITISH WERE FORCED TO TAKE COVER.

BUT THIS WAS ONLY A SHORT RESPITE.

I'VE DECIDED NOT TO SURRENDER. THOSE WHO WANT TO DIE MAY REMAIN WITH ME. OTHERS MAY LEAVE THE FORT.

YOU ARE A BRAVE WOMAN. I WILL STAND BY YOU. WE'LL LEAVE THE CITY TO-NIGHT AND JOIN RAO SAHEB AT KALPI.

AT MIDNIGHT...

THE RANI OF JHANSI HAS ESCAPED!

LET'S GIVE CHASE!

WE'LL NEVER CATCH UP WITH HER!

SHE'S KILLED TWO SOLDIERS WHO TRIED TO CAPTURE HER!

THE BRITISH HAVE DESTROYED JHANSI!

THEY HAVE EVEN WRECKED THE STATE LIBRARY!

WHY? WHAT WRONG HAVE THE PEOPLE OF JHANSI DONE?

THE BRITISH SAY THEY WANT TO TEACH THE CITY A LESSON AND SET AN EXAMPLE SO THAT NONE WILL AGAIN DARE TO CHALLENGE THEM!

LAKSHMIBAI RODE INTO RAO SAHEB'S CAMP AT KALPI.

WELCOME BRAVE WARRIOR. I NEED YOUR SUPPORT IN MY STRUGGLE.

NOTHING WILL GIVE ME GREATER HAPPINESS THAN TO DIE ON THE BATTLE-FIELD SERVING THE MARATHA STANDARD!

I WOULD LIKE YOU TO INSPECT THE TROOPS.

YOU MUST HAVE STRICT DISCIPLINE IN THE RANKS. THERE SHOULD BE MILITARY DRILL AND EXERCISES EVERY MORNING.

THE BRITISH ARE PLANNING A SIEGE ON KALPI!

LET'S GO OUT AND MEET THEM AT KOONCH.

THAT'S A GOOD IDEA. WE'LL FACE THEM IN THE OPEN.

WE MUST HAVE A STRONG REARGUARD!

WE'RE ALL VETERANS IN THE ART OF WAR! LET THE BRITISH COME!

BUT THE OVER-CONFIDENT NATIONALIST LEADERS DID NOT HEED LAKSHMIBAI'S COUNSEL ABOUT A STRONG REARGUARD AND RAO SAHEB'S ARMY WAS ROUTED.

ALL IS LOST! LET'S FLEE!

THERE IS NO HOPE NOW. WE MIGHT AS WELL SURRENDER!

WE'VE BEEN UTTERLY DEFEATED!

DON'T LOSE HEART. THE NAWAB OF BANDA HAS JUST ARRIVED WITH A FORCE OF 2,000 CAVALRY, GUNS AND INFANTRY!

RAO SAHEB HELD A COUNCIL OF WAR TO CONSIDER THEIR NEXT MOVE.

OUR SITUATION IS BECOMING WORSE EVERY HOUR. WHAT SHOULD WE DO?

WE'LL FIGHT TO THE LAST MAN.

WE SHOULD FIGHT TO THE END. WE CAN STILL RETRIEVE OUR HONOUR IF WE OFFER A DETERMINED RESISTANCE AND THE TROOPS OBSERVE DISCIPLINE.

BUT THE CLEVER STRATEGY OF THE BRITISH AGAIN WON THE DAY AND RAO SAHEB'S ARMY FLED IN CONFUSION.

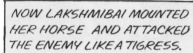

NOW LAKSHMIBAI MOUNTED HER HORSE AND ATTACKED THE ENEMY LIKE A TIGRESS.

HER EXAMPLE ENCOURAGED THE OTHER LEADERS WHO NOW DASHED FORWARD TO JOIN THE ATTACK.

COME ON! VICTORY WILL BE OURS!

FOLLOW THE RANI OF JHANSI! THE ENEMIES ARE RETREATING!

THEN SIR HUGH ROSE, THE BRITISH GENERAL, ORDERED THE CAMEL CORPS TO CHARGE.

THE PESHWA'S MEN, UNABLE TO WITHSTAND THE ATTACK, FELL BACK IN CONFUSION.

THE REVOLUTIONARY SPIRIT WAS NOW COMPLETELY SHATTERED. THE BRITISH TOOK OVER THE FORT OF KALPI ON MAY 24, 1858 WITHOUT FURTHER FIGHTING.

THE NATIONALIST CHIEFS HELD ANOTHER CONFERENCE.

ALL CHANCES OF VICTORY ARE AT AN END!

WE CAN HARASS THE ENEMY BY GUERRILLA WARFARE.

THAT'S AN EXCELLENT PLAN!

THAT WAS POSSIBLE FOR THE MARATHAS BECAUSE THEY POSSESSED UNCONQUERABLE FORTRESSES. WE CANNOT FIGHT WITHOUT A STRONG FORT.

I THINK WE SHOULD MARCH TO GWALIOR AND OBTAIN THE HELP OF THE MAHARAJA. WITH THAT FORT IN OUR HANDS WE CAN STILL CARRY ON THE WAR AND WIN.

I AGREE. THOUGH HE IS AN ALLY OF THE BRITISH, HIS PEOPLE ARE ON OUR SIDE.

HAS THE MAHARAJA OF GWALIOR AGREED TO GIVE US MONEY AND SUPPLIES?

NO! HE HAS ORDERED HIS TROOPS TO ATTACK US.

THE SIGHT OF LAKSHMIBAI WAS ENOUGH TO MAKE THE GWALIOR ARMY DROP THEIR GUNS.

LOOK! IT'S THE RANI OF JHANSI!

HAIL, RANI OF JHANSI!

VICTORY TO LAKSHMIBAI!

RAO SAHEB ENTERED GWALIOR IN TRIUMPH AND HELD A GRAND DURBAR TO PROCLAIM HIS LEADERSHIP OF THE MARATHA CONFEDERACY.

RAO SAHEB HAS SAVED THE HONOUR OF INDIA!

LONG LIVE THE PESHWA!

AS THE CEREMONIES CONTINUED, LAKSHMIBAI GREW IMPATIENT.

WE HAVE FUNDS, AND A WELL-EQUIPPED ARMY. WE SHOULD PREPARE FOR THE NEXT STRUGGLE.

WE HAVE PLENTY OF TIME.

SO WHEN THE BRITISH MARCHED ON GWALIOR RAO SAHEB WAS TOTALLY UNPREPARED.

THE BRITISH HAVE ALREADY BEGUN TO ATTACK!

AND OUR ARMY IS NOT READY. TAKE YOUR TROOPS OUT FOR ONE LAST GLORIOUS ATTACK. I AM READY TO DO MY DUTY. YOU DO YOURS! GOD BE WITH YOU!

LAKSHMIBAI DRESSED IN A MAN'S GARB ADVANCED TO ATTACK THE ENEMY.

BRITISH RE-
INFORCEMENTS
HAVE
ARRIVED!
ALL IS
LOST!

I WILL
NOT LOSE
HOPE! I WILL
NEVER
SURRENDER!

THE ARMIES WERE EVENLY MATCHED.

FORWARD!
COME ON!

SO ENDED THE LIFE OF INDIA'S GREATEST HEROINE IN THE STRUGGLE FOR FREEDOM.

TIPU SULTAN

THE TIGER OF MYSORE

The route to your roots

TIPU SULTAN

Tipu Sultan died as he had lived – a free man. A childhood spent watching and helping in his father's campaigns had made him a shrewd general. From his father he also inherited courage and a sense of honour and, most importantly, the determination to oust the British from Indian soil. But this noble 18th-century warrior had no weapon against treachery.

Script	Illustrations	Editor
Subba Rao	G.R.Naik	Anant Pai

TIPU SULTAN

PLACE: DEVANAHALLI.* YEAR: 1750. HAIDAR ALI, AN OFFICER OF THE MYSORE ARMY, WAS RETURNING HOME WITH HIS TRUSTED FRIEND, KHANDE RAO, AFTER A SUCCESSFUL CAMPAIGN.

AS HAIDAR ALI RODE UP TO HIS HOME, HE WAS GREETED WITH GOOD NEWS—

THE BEGUM SAHIBA HAS GIVEN BIRTH TO A SON!

PRAISED BE ALLAH!

MY SON LOOKS STRONG AND HANDSOME, DOESN'T HE, KHANDE RAO?

YES, HAIDAR. HE WILL GROW UP TO BE A GREAT SOLDIER LIKE YOU.

1

THE BOY WAS NAMED TIPU SULTAN. HE SPENT HIS CHILDHOOD AT DINDIGUL, WHERE HAIDAR WAS APPOINTED COMMANDER.

LET US PLAY 'TIGER AND THE SHEEP'. I WILL BE THE TIGER!

YOU CAN'T BE THE TIGER EVERY TIME. LET ME BE THE TIGER THIS TIME.

TIPU DIDN'T AGREE. SO —

LET ME GO. YOU CAN BE THE TIGER FOREVER.

HAIDAR HAD TO GO ON FREQUENT EXPEDITIONS AGAINST ERRING FEUDAL CHIEFS. ON ONE SUCH OCCASION —

FATHER, WHO ARE THE MOST POWERFUL OF ALL THE ENEMIES YOU HAVE FOUGHT?

THE BRITISH ARE THE MOST DANGEROUS ENEMIES OF MYSORE — AND OF HINDUSTAN.

AND I WILL DRIVE THEM OUT OF INDIA WITH ALLAH'S HELP.

TIPU SOLEMNLY PROMISED HIS FATHER.

AND I WILL HELP YOU, FATHER. COUNT ON ME.

WHEN TIPU WAS TEN YEARS OLD, HAIDAR LEFT FOR THE CAPITAL, SRIRANGA PATTANA, TO ASSUME COMMAND OF THE STATE ARMY.

AT THE CAPITAL HAIDAR FORCED THE DALWAI,* NANJARAJ, TO RETIRE AND ASSUMED THE POST HIMSELF. BUT HIS SUCCESS WAS SHORT-LIVED. TROUBLE CAME FROM AN UNEXPECTED QUARTER.

MY LORD! KHANDE RAO HAS TAKEN CHARGE OF THE FORT!

KHANDE RAO? MY FRIEND HAS BETRAYED ME!

WHEN HAIDAR'S WIFE CAME TO KNOW OF KHANDE RAO'S TREACHERY —

YOU HAD BETTER ESCAPE NOW, BEFORE YOU ARE CAPTURED.

I CAN'T LEAVE YOU AT THE MERCY OF KHANDE RAO.

DON'T WORRY ABOUT US, FATHER. I'LL LOOK AFTER MOTHER. YOU GO NOW AND COME BACK WITH A BIG ARMY TO DEFEAT KHANDE RAO.

HAIDAR LEFT RELUCTANTLY.

SECONDS AFTER THIS, KHANDE RAO'S SOLDIERS RODE UP.

STOP! ANYONE WHO DARES CROSS THIS THRESHOLD WILL PAY WITH HIS LIFE!

KHANDE RAO, WHO HAD JUST COME, SAW THIS.

MOVE ON — ALL OF YOU! EVEN IN CAPTIVITY A TIGER SHOULD NOT BE TRIFLED WITH.

KHANDE RAO TOOK HAIDAR'S FAMILY INTO THE FORT AS CAPTIVES, BUT HE TREATED THEM WELL.

HAIDAR SOON RETURNED WITH A STRONG ARMY AND DEFEATED KHANDE RAO.

PUT THIS TRAITOR INTO THE DUNGEONS.

ALTHOUGH HAIDAR WAS NOW VIRTUALLY THE RULER, HE CONTINUED TO PAY RESPECT TO THE TITULAR KING. HIS IMMEDIATE TASK WAS TO STRENGTHEN THE ARMY.

FATHER, I WOULD LIKE TO FIGHT BY YOUR SIDE. MAY I?

YES, MY SON. BUT YOU MUST FIRST RECEIVE TRAINING.

TIPU WAS SENT TO BIDANUR WHERE HE BEGAN HIS TRAINING. HE ALSO LEARNT PERSIAN, ARABIC, KANNADA AND SANSKRIT.

GOOD SHOT!

TIPU WAS JUST FIFTEEN WHEN HE HAD HIS FIRST TASTE OF WAR. HE ACCOMPANIED HIS FATHER IN A CAMPAIGN AGAINST THE RULER OF BALAM.*

I'LL CHARGE WITH THE MAIN ARMY. TIPU, YOU TAKE COMMAND OF THE REAR.

YES, FATHER.

HAIDAR RODE AWAY, WHILE TIPU WAITED IMPATIENTLY FOR HIS RETURN.

NO NEWS OF FATHER! I'LL JOIN HIM WITH MY MEN. HE MAY NEED MY HELP.

AVOIDING THE DIRECT ROUTE, HE LED HIS MEN THROUGH THE FOREST.

SUDDENLY —

WOMEN AND CHILDREN HERE! THEN THIS MUST BE THE HIDEOUT OF THE BALAM RULER'S WOMEN-FOLK!

HE HAD THEM SURROUNDED AND TAKEN CAPTIVE.

HAVE NO FEAR. YOU'LL COME TO NO HARM IF YOU STAY QUIETLY IN YOUR TENTS.

MAY GOD BLESS YOU, SON.

WHEN THE NEWS OF THE CAPTURE OF HIS HAREM REACHED THE RULER OF BALAM —

I SURRENDER. PLEASE RELEASE THE MEMBERS OF MY HOUSEHOLD WHO HAVE BEEN CAPTURED BY YOUR SON.

HAIDAR WAS PERPLEXED.

CAPTURED BY TIPU?

HE TURNED TO ONE OF HIS COMMANDERS.

MAQBOOL KHAN, PLEASE FIND OUT IF THIS IS TRUE.

I'LL SEND ONE OF MY MEN TO GUIDE YOU THROUGH THE FOREST.

SOON MAQBOOL KHAN ARRIVED WHERE TIPU HAD CAMPED.

WELL DONE, TIPU! THE ENEMY HAS SURRENDERED.

THEN WE CAN RELEASE THE PRISONERS....

BEFORE HE COULD FINISH SPEAKING, MAQBOOL KHAN RUSHED INTO THE TENT AND...

WHERE ARE YOU GOING?

...CAME OUT DRAGGING THE FRIGHTENED WIFE OF THE RULER OF BALAM.

MAQBOOL KHAN! RELEASE HER!

IGNORING YOUNG TIPU'S ANGUISHED CRY, MAQBOOL CONTINUED TO DRAG HER.

IF YOU DON'T RELEASE HER, MAQBOOL, I'LL SHOOT YOU!

BUT MAQBOOL DID NOT HEED HIS THREAT.

THEN —

BANG

LATER, WHEN HAIDAR JOINED HIS SON —

FATHER! I HAD TO KILL MAQBOOL.

I UNDERSTAND. WOMEN AND CHILDREN MUST BE PROTECTED AND TREATED WITH RESPECT.

FATHER AND SON RETURNED TO SRIRANGA PATTANA IN TRIUMPH.

IN 1767, HAIDAR DECLARED WAR ON THE BRITISH.

FATHER, WE ARE CERTAIN TO WIN.

HOW CAN WE BE SURE OF VICTORY? REMEMBER, THE NIZAM OF HYDERABAD IS ON THE SIDE OF THE BRITISH — SO ARE THE MARATHAS.

IF ONLY ALL THE RULERS OF HINDUSTAN WOULD UNITE . . . .

FATHER, WHY DON'T WE TRY TO WIN THEM OVER?

WE COULD TRY . . . .

HAIDAR OPENED NEGOTIATIONS WITH THE NIZAM AND WON HIM OVER. HE SENT TIPU TO THE NIZAM'S CAMP TO SIGN THE TREATY.

A TIGER ENTERING THE LION'S DEN!

THE NIZAM RECEIVED HIM WITH COURTESY.

THE BRITISH STAND TO GAIN BY THE HOSTILITY BETWEEN US. LET US UNITE AND FIGHT AGAINST THE FOREIGNERS, OUR COMMON ENEMY.

HE SOUNDS EARNEST....

PRINCE, TELL YOUR FATHER THAT MY ARMY IS AT HIS DISPOSAL. WE WILL FIGHT TOGETHER AGAINST THE BRITISH.

WE ARE GRATE-FUL FOR YOUR TIMELY SUPPORT.

AND, TIPU, YOU ARE THE FORTUNE OF YOUR STATE — NASIB-UD-DAULAH.

TIPU RETURNED TO SRIRANGA PATTANA, HAPPY AT HIS SUCCESS WITH THE NIZAM. HIS FATHER HAD GOOD NEWS FOR HIM TOO.

I'VE HEARD FROM THE PESHWA. HE HAS AGREED TO REMAIN NEUTRAL

FOR ONCE THE BRITISH HAVE FAILED TO DIVIDE US, FATHER.

A FIERCE WAR WHICH WENT ON FOR TWO YEARS ENSUED WITH THE BRITISH.

ALTHOUGH THE FICKLE NIZAM WITHDREW HIS SUPPORT, HAIDAR ADVANCED STEADILY AND ULTIMATELY REACHED THE VERY GATES OF MADRAS, THE BRITISH HEADQUARTERS IN SOUTH INDIA.

THERE HAIDAR DICTATED HIS PEACE TERMS TO THE BRITISH.

WE ACCEPT YOUR CONDITIONS.

IN THAT CASE, HOSTILITIES WILL CEASE AT ONCE.

BUT BARELY SIX MONTHS AFTER THIS, HAIDAR HAD TO FACE THE MARATHAS.

HAIDAR WAS BEATEN AND HAD TO FLEE WITH THE MAIN ARMY.

FOR A WHILE TIPU, WITH A SMALL BAND OF MEN, TRIED TO HOLD THE MARATHAS AT BAY.

BUT IT WAS OF NO USE. A LITTLE LATER —

PRINCE, LET US ESCAPE BEFORE WE ARE OVER-POWERED.

ALL RIGHT, SAYYID.

TIPU AND SAYYID MUHAMMED RODE AWAY SWIFTLY, LEAVING THE PURSUING ENEMY FAR BEHIND.

MEANWHILE HAIDAR, WHO HAD MANAGED TO REACH THE CAPITAL, WAS PRAYING.

ALLAH, TAKE CARE OF TIPU. KEEP HIM SAFE FROM HARM.

JUST THEN TWO MENDICANTS CALLED ON HAIDAR.

HOLY ONES, WILL I SEE MY SON ALIVE?

CERTAINLY, YOU WILL.

THE NEXT MOMENT —

MY SON!

LATER HAIDAR REGAINED THE TERRITORIES LOST TO THE MARATHAS.

ALL WAS QUIET FOR A WHILE. DURING THIS PERIOD TIPU GOT MARRIED. ONE DAY TIPU AND A FRENCH CAPTAIN, WHO WAS EMPLOYED BY HAIDAR TO TRAIN HIS SOLDIERS, WERE RETURNING FROM A HUNTING EXPEDITION.

LOOK!

A TIGER!

AS THE FRENCHMAN PREPARED TO SHOOT —

STOP! WE DON'T HUNT TIGERS THAT WAY IN HINDUSTAN. LEAVE HIM TO ME.

EVEN AS THE TIGER PREPARED TO POUNCE UPON HIM, TIPU DREW HIS SWORD.

BRAVO!

THE SLAIN TIGER WAS TAKEN OUT IN A PROCESSION THROUGH THE STREETS OF SRIRANGA PATTANA.

TIPU! HE IS THE TIGER OF MYSORE!

VICTORY TO THE TIGER OF MYSORE!

IN 1780, HAIDAR DECLARED WAR ON THE BRITISH AGAIN. FIERCE BATTLES WERE FOUGHT AT VARIOUS PLACES.

TIPU HAD BEEN SENT TO MALABAR TO DEFEND IT AGAINST THE BRITISH. HE WAS CAMPING AT PONNANI WHEN —

PRINCE, I HAVE SAD NEWS. YOUR FATHER DIED AT NARASINGA-RAYANA PATTANA.

TIPU IMMEDIATELY LEFT PONNANI.

15

PURNAIYA, A MINISTER, MET HIM WELL BEFORE HE HAD REACHED HIS DESTINATION.

BY GOD'S GRACE WE HAVE BEEN ABLE TO FOIL THE CONSPIRACY TO DEPRIVE YOU OF THE OFFICE OF DALWAI. THE TRAITORS HAVE BEEN IMPRISONED. HERE IS A LIST OF THEIR NAMES.

CONSPIRACY? AGAINST ME?

TIPU BECAME THOUGHTFUL

I THOUGHT OUR PEOPLE LOVED ME, THAT THEY WANTED ME. I DON'T WANT TO SET OFF AN ENDLESS CHAIN OF KILLING. I'LL BECOME AN ASCETIC.

WHEN TIPU TOLD PURNAIYA OF HIS DECISION —

NO, TIPU, MY SON! IF A FEW SELFISH AND THOUGHTLESS MEN ARE AGAINST YOU, MILLIONS OF OTHERS ARE BEHIND YOU. DON'T DISAPPOINT THEM.

THE DEVOTED MINISTER CONTINUED TO PLEAD —

TIPU, YOU ARE OUR ONLY HOPE AGAINST THE BRITISH. THE PEOPLE NEED YOU.

AT LAST, TIPU YIELDED.

ALL RIGHT, I GIVE IN.

THEN HE TORE THE LIST INTO PIECES.

ALL THE SAME, I PARDON ALL THE CONSPIRATORS. I AM AT WAR WITH THE BRITISH, NOT WITH MY OWN PEOPLE.

TIPU, MY LORD!

TIPU AND PURNAIYA RESUMED THEIR JOURNEY. ON REACHING CHITTOOR* WHERE HAIDAR'S ARMY HAD ENCAMPED, TIPU WAS DECLARED HAIDAR'S SUCCESSOR.

MEANWHILE, THE BRITISH WERE HAPPY AT THE NEWS OF HAIDAR'S DEATH, AND AN ARMY UNDER GENERAL MATTHEWS SET SAIL FROM BOMBAY FOR THE SOUTH.

NOW THAT HAIDAR IS DEAD, WE'LL TAKE MYSORE.

IT'LL BE EASY. TIPU IS YOUNG AND INEXPERIENCED.

* NOT TO BE CONFUSED WITH CHITTOR OF RAJASTHAN.

GENERAL MATTHEWS OCCUPIED BIDANUR, A FORT NEAR MANGALORE. TIPU IMMEDIATELY WENT TO THE RESCUE AND BESIEGED THE FORT.

AFTER EIGHTEEN DAYS, GENERAL MATTHEWS SUED FOR PEACE.

GENERAL MATTHEWS WILL SURRENDER THE FORT BUT HE MUST BE GRANTED SAFE CONDUCT THROUGH YOUR TERRITORY.

I AGREE, ON ONE CONDITION. NOTHING VALUABLE SHOULD BE TAKEN FROM BIDANUR.

DESPITE TIPU'S WARNING, MATTHEWS THREW OPEN THE TREASURY IN THE FORT TO HIS SOLDIERS.

HELP YOURSELVES, LADS!

THEN THE BRITISH ARMY MARCHED OUT OF THE FORT...

...AND DEPOSITED THEIR ARMS BEFORE TIPU'S SOLDIERS AS A TOKEN OF SURRENDER.

TRUE TO HIS WORD, TIPU ALLOWED THE BRITISH TO GO. SECONDS LATER —

THE TREASURY IS EMPTY.

STOP THE BRITISH AT ONCE AND SEARCH THEM.

EVERY BRITISH KNAPSACK WAS FOUND TO BE LINED WITH GOLD AND JEWELS. TIPU BECAME VERY ANGRY.

GENERAL MATTHEWS, YOU HAVE VIOLATED OUR AGREEMENT. YOU AND YOUR SOLDIERS HAVE ACTED LIKE COMMON THIEVES! YOU HAVE FORFEITED THE RIGHT TO BE TREATED AS GENTLEMEN. YOU WILL BE TAKEN PRISONER.

TIPU THEN PROCEEDED TO LAY SIEGE TO MANGALORE WHICH WAS AT THAT TIME OCCUPIED BY THE BRITISH.

WHEN THE FALL OF MANGALORE WAS IMMINENT, THE BRITISH SIGNED A PEACE TREATY WITH HIM.

WE AGREE TO RESTORE YOUR TERRITORIES OCCUPIED BY US.

TIPU RETURNED TO SRIRANGA PATTANA AND WORKED FOR THE WELFARE OF HIS PEOPLE. ONE DAY TWO BRAHMANS FROM SRINGERI CALLED ON HIM —

THE TEMPLE OF GODDESS SHARADA HAS BEEN RANSACKED BY SOME MISCREANTS.

I AM GRIEVED TO HEAR THIS. PEOPLE DO EVIL DEEDS WITH A SMILE ONLY TO SUFFER THE CONSEQUENCES WITH TEARS.

HE SENT GOLD AND JEWELS TO SRINGERI FOR THE CONSECRATION OF GODDESS SHARADA.

LATER, THE BRAHMANS CAME AGAIN, BRINGING HIM THE HOLY OFFERING.

PRAY FOR THE PROSPERITY OF MY PEOPLE.

MEANWHILE, CORNWALLIS, THE BRITISH GOVERNOR-GENERAL IN CALCUTTA, WAS WORRIED ABOUT THE GROWING POWER OF TIPU.

TIPU SHOULD BE CUT DOWN TO SIZE.

OUR REPEATED EFFORTS TO HUMBLE TIPU HAVE BEEN FUTILE.

UNAWARE OF THE BRITISH CONSPIRACY AGAINST HIM, TIPU WAS RELAXING IN HIS GARDEN, WATCHING HIS TWO YOUNG SONS PLAY.

GOOD, ABDUL! COME ON, MUIZ-UD-DIN, THROW HIM OFF.

ABBAJAN, WE ARE NOW READY TO TAKE ON THE BRITISH.

ABBAJAN, TELL US, WHEN WILL WE HAVE ANOTHER WAR WITH THEM?

JUST THEN A MESSENGER ARRIVED.

YOUR MAJESTY, THE BRITISH, THE NIZAM AND THE MARATHAS HAVE JOINTLY DECLARED WAR ON US.

SO MY OWN COUNTRYMEN ARE UNITING WITH THE FOREIGNERS! I ACCEPT THE CHALLENGE.

WAR BROKE OUT. TIPU LOST FORT AFTER FORT.

BANGALORE IS LOST!

WE WILL RETREAT TO THE CAPITAL AND WILL FIGHT THEM THERE.

WHEN THE BRITISH ARMY FINALLY REACHED THE GATES OF SRIRANGA PATTANA, TIPU AND HIS SOLDIERS FOUGHT DESPERATELY . . .

. . . AND COMPELLED CORNWALLIS TO RETREAT.

WE WILL COME BACK AFTER THE PESHWA'S ARMY JOINS US.

WHILE CORNWALLIS' ARMY WAS RETREATING TO BANGALORE —

MY GOD! TIPU'S RIDERS!

WE'LL BE CAUGHT BETWEEN HIS TWO ARMIES!

BUT IT TURNED OUT TO BE THE PESHWA'S ARMY COMING TO HELP CORNWALLIS.

I'M GRATEFUL TO YOU, HARIPANT, FOR YOUR TIMELY HELP.

THE BATTLE WAS RESUMED AND TIPU WAS COMPELLED TO SUE FOR PEACE.

FIRST, WE MUST GET OUT OF THIS PREDICAMENT. I'LL HAVE MY REVENGE LATER.

TIPU SENT HIS ENVOYS TO THE BRITISH, WHO AGREED TO CEASE FIGHTING. BUT THEIR TERMS OF PEACE WERE VERY HARSH.

THE BRITISH WANT THREE CRORES AND THIRTY LAKHS OF RUPEES AS WAR EXPENSES. IN ADDITION, THEY WANT HALF YOUR KINGDOM.

CONVEY MY ACCEPTANCE OF THE TERMS TO CORNWALLIS.

THEY MAKE ONE MORE DEMAND — THEY WILL KEEP YOUR TWO YOUNG SONS AS HOSTAGES, TILL ALL THE TERMS OF THE TREATY ARE HONOURED.

THE BLACKGUARDS! HOWEVER, WAR IS WAR. PREPARE MY SONS FOR THEIR DEPARTURE, GHULAM ALI.

ON THE DAY TIPU'S SONS WERE TO BE SENT OVER TO THE BRITISH —

ABBAJAN!

CHILDREN, DON'T LOSE HEART. YOU ARE TIGER CUBS, AREN'T YOU? DON'T EVER FORGET THAT!

YES, ABBAJAN.

THE PEOPLE OF SRIRANGA PATTANA, WHO THRONGED THE STREETS TO BID THEM FAREWELL, WERE FILLED WITH PITY FOR THE YOUNG BOYS.

HOW CALM THEY LOOK, THE POOR DARLINGS!

THEY DON'T LOOK A BIT AFRAID!

THEY ARE, AFTER ALL, TIPU'S SONS!

THE PEACE TREATY WAS CONCLUDED.

THIS IS ONLY A TRUCE. THERE WILL BE NO REAL PEACE TILL THE BRITISH LEAVE HINDUSTAN.

THE PEOPLE OF MYSORE VOLUNTEERED TO PAY A SPECIAL TAX TO SPEED UP THE PAYMENT OF WAR DAMAGES.

THE SULTAN WILL APPRECIATE YOUR GESTURE.

FINALLY THE TERMS OF THE TREATY WERE FULFILLED, AND THE PRINCES RETURNED. TIPU THEN TURNED HIS FULL ATTENTION TO STRENGTHENING HIS ARMY.

LORD WELLESLEY, WHO HAD BEEN APPOINTED THE GOVERNOR-GENERAL OF BRITISH INDIA, WAS NOT IDLE, EITHER.

WE COULD BE THE PARAMOUNT POWER IN INDIA — THE ONLY OBSTACLE IS TIPU.

THAT MAN IS WILY. HIS LATEST MOVE HAS BEEN TO SEND AMBASSADORS TO AFGHANISTAN, IRAN AND FRANCE ASKING FOR MILITARY HELP...

. . . AND NAPOLEON MAY WELL DECIDE TO SAIL FROM EGYPT TO INDIA, IN RESPONSE TO TIPU'S CALL FOR HELP.

NELSON WILL TAKE CARE OF NAPOLEON. I'LL HANDLE TIPU.

UNDER GENERAL HARRIS, THE COMBINED ARMY OF THE BRITISH AND THE NIZAM BESIEGED SRIRANGA PATTANA. THIS TIME THE PESHWA DID NOT JOIN THEM.

THE FORT WAS UNDER CONSTANT FIRE, WHICH IT WITHSTOOD MAGNIFICENTLY.

LET THEM TRY THEIR BEST. I AM READY FOR THEM.

THE BRITISH SIDE WAS DEFINITELY GETTING THE WORST OF IT.

WE HAVE RUN OUT OF SUPPLIES, BAIRD. THE FORT MUST BE TAKEN WITHOUT DELAY.

BUT THIS FORT IS IMPREGNABLE!

NO FORT IS IMPREGNABLE SO LONG AS TRAITORS CAN BE FOUND IN IT.

THEY FOUND THEIR MAN IN MIR SADIQ, A GENERAL WHOM TIPU TRUSTED IMPLICITLY.

REMEMBER MIR SADIQ'S ADVICE — CONCENTRATE ON THE NORTH-EASTERN WALL.

THE BRITISH SUCCEEDED IN MAKING A SMALL BREACH IN THE ONE WEAK SPOT OF THE FORT.

TIPU WENT TO INSPECT THE WALL.

IT IS ONLY A TINY GAP, YOUR MAJESTY. I'LL HAVE IT REPAIRED AT ONCE.

I AM NOT WORRIED, MIR SADIQ. THE NORTH-EASTERN SIDE IS IN YOUR CAPABLE HANDS.

THAT NIGHT, THE BRITISH SECRETLY MADE TRENCHES OUTSIDE THE NORTH-EASTERN WALL AND HID THERE.

THE NEXT AFTERNOON, INSIDE THE FORT —

I DON'T FORESEE AN ATTACK ON THIS SIDE TODAY. YOU MAY ALL GO TO THE TREASURY FOR YOUR PAY.

THEN MIR SADIQ WAVED A PIECE OF CLOTH AS A SIGNAL TO THE BRITISH THAT THE COAST WAS CLEAR.

TIPU WAS DIRECTING OPERATIONS ON THE NORTHERN FRONT.

EVERYTHING IS UNDER CONTROL, SULTAN.

GOOD!

LUNCH WAS LAID OUT UNDER THE SHADE OF A MANGO TREE. TIPU SAT DOWN TO HAVE A QUICK MEAL.

HE HAD BARELY HAD A MORSEL OR TWO WHEN —

WE HAVE BEEN BETRAYED BY MIR SADIQ! THE BRITISH SOLDIERS ARE POURING IN.

TIPU HASTENED TO THE NORTH-EAST.

BUT THE BRITISH HAD ALREADY HOISTED THEIR FLAG.
TIPU FOUGHT HIS WAY TO THE BREACH.

A FOREIGN FLAG ON MY FORT! I WON'T ALLOW THAT!

TIPU WAS SURROUNDED BY BRITISH SOLDIERS, WHO DID NOT KNOW WHO HE WAS. HE FOUGHT DESPERATELY...

...AND FELL AS A BULLET STRUCK HIM ON THE CHEST.

ONE OF THE BRITISH TRIED TO SEIZE HIS SWORD-BELT BUT TIPU, WOUNDED AS HE WAS, STRUCK HIM.

THE ENRAGED SOLDIER SHOT HIM THROUGH THE TEMPLE.

AND THE TIGER FELL DEAD.

LATER, THE BRITISH DISCOVERED WHO HE WAS.

TIPU WAS BURIED WITH HONOUR BESIDE HIS FATHER. TO ADD TO THE SOLEMNITY OF THE SCENE, THE DAY ENDED WITH A MOST DREADFUL THUNDERSTORM.

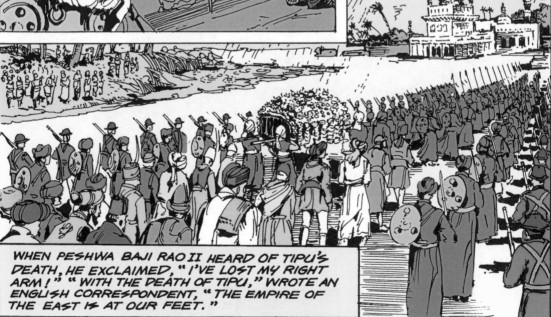

WHEN PESHWA BAJI RAO II HEARD OF TIPU'S DEATH, HE EXCLAIMED, "I'VE LOST MY RIGHT ARM!" "WITH THE DEATH OF TIPU," WROTE AN ENGLISH CORRESPONDENT, "THE EMPIRE OF THE EAST IS AT OUR FEET."

VELU THAMPI

THE COURAGEOUS DIWAN OF TRAVANCORE

The route to your roots

VELU THAMPI

It was a time of corruption and despotism in the state of Travancore. Balarama Varma, the Maharaja, was a helpless teenager who watched his Diwan take advantage of his inexperience to impose crushing taxes on the people and pocket the money himself. It was Velu Thampi who led a rebellion and overthrew the Diwan. The grateful Maharaja proclaimed him the Diwan and the people enjoyed a period of justice and firm administration. But then a greater foe awaited Velu Thampi – the British East India Company, which had begun to interfere in the internal affairs of Travancore.

Script
Radha M.Nair

Illustrations
M.Mohandas

Editor
Anant Pai

VELU THAMPI

VELU THAMPI STARTED HIS CAREER AS A TEHSILDAR IN THE KINGDOM OF TRAVANCORE* DURING THE REIGN OF MAHARAJA BALARAMA VARMA.

* NOW PART OF KERALA

IT WAS AN UNHAPPY TIME FOR THE PEOPLE OF TRAVANCORE. UNJUST TAXES HAD RUINED THEM.

OH, PLEASE, DON'T TAKE MY ENTIRE HARVEST AS LEVY!

WE HAVE TO CARRY OUT THE ORDERS OF THE DIWAN.*

THE DIWAN WAS RUTHLESS AND OPPRESSED THE PEOPLE. THE MAHARAJA COULD NOT CHECK HIM. HE WAS ONLY SIXTEEN YEARS OLD AND WAS IN THE DIWAN'S CHARGE.

YOU DARE TO OPPOSE THE DIWAN'S WILL? TAKE THAT — AND THAT!

THE DIWAN BEGAN TO USURP SOME OF THE MAHARAJA'S PRIVILEGES.

BRING THE MAHARAJA'S PERSONAL PALANQUIN TO ME AT ONCE! I WISH TO GO OUT IN IT!

VERY WELL, SIR.

* PRIME MINISTER

VELU THAMPI SAW THE DIWAN IN THE MAHARAJA'S PALANQUIN. HE TURNED TO HIS BROTHER, PADMANABHAN.

ISN'T THAT THE ROYAL PALANQUIN? WHO'S BEING CARRIED IN IT?

IT'S THE DIWAN, JAYANTHAN SANKARAN NAMBOODIRI.

THE ARROGANCE OF THE DIWAN INCENSED VELU THAMPI.

HALT THE PALANQUIN AT ONCE!

BROTHER, BE CAREFUL HOW YOU SPEAK TO THE DIWAN!

THE DIWAN HAS NO RIGHT TO RIDE IN THIS PALANQUIN!

YOU'LL PAY FOR THIS, VELU THAMPI.

IT IS YOU WHO WILL SOON HAVE TO PAY FOR YOUR GREED AND CORRUPTION!

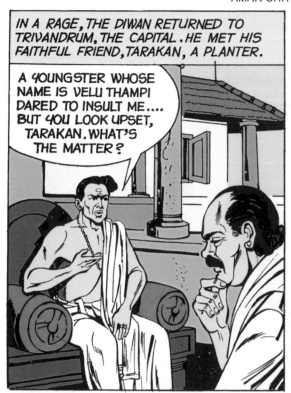

IN A RAGE, THE DIWAN RETURNED TO TRIVANDRUM, THE CAPITAL. HE MET HIS FAITHFUL FRIEND, TARAKAN, A PLANTER.

A YOUNGSTER WHOSE NAME IS VELU THAMPI DARED TO INSULT ME.... BUT YOU LOOK UPSET, TARAKAN. WHAT'S THE MATTER?

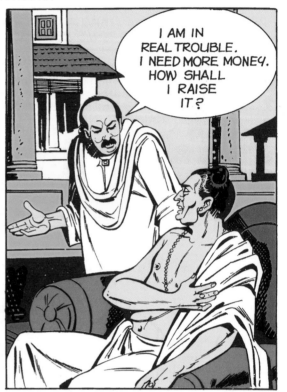

I AM IN REAL TROUBLE. I NEED MORE MONEY. HOW SHALL I RAISE IT?

HA! HA! THAT'S SIMPLE! WE SHALL JUST LEVY SOME MORE TAXES!

GOOD IDEA! LET THE PEOPLE PAY FOR OUR PLEASURES!

AFTER ALL, WE ENJOY THE SUPPORT OF THE BRITISH RESIDENT, MACAULAY. EVEN THE MAHARAJA DOES HIS BIDDING. SO WE NEED FEAR NO ONE.

I'LL SPEAK TO HIS HIGHNESS AT ONCE.

VELU THAMPI

5

WE WILL DEMAND THAT THE DIWAN BE REPLACED!

WE SHALL PETITION THE MAHARAJA.

SO THEY WENT WITH VELU THAMPI TO TRIVANDRUM.

THEN THEY DESCRIBED THE PEOPLE'S PLIGHT TO THE MAHARAJA.

YOUR HIGHNESS, WE HAVE BEEN CRUSHED BY THE TYRANNY OF THE DIWAN. HE MUST BE REMOVED FROM OFFICE.

YOU ARE RIGHT. I HAD NOT REALISED HOW DEEP-ROOTED THE CORRUPTION WAS.

I HEREBY ORDER THAT THE DIWAN BE REMOVED FROM OFFICE. I ORDER THAT HIS EARS BE CUT OFF, AND THAT HE SHOULD BE EXILED.

AND YOU, VELU THAMPI, SHALL BE MY NEW DIWAN.

I AM HONOURED YOUR HIGHNESS.

I SHALL DO MY BEST TO SERVE THE MAHARAJA AND MY COUNTRY.

LONG LIVE THE NEW DIWAN!

THE FORMER DIWAN WAS ARRESTED.

WHAT IS THE MEANING OF THIS?

WE ARE ONLY CARRYING OUT THE MAHARAJA'S ORDERS.

HE DESERVES THE PUNISHMENT!

TARAKAN FLED TO THE BRITISH RESIDENT FOR HELP.

I AM RUINED. YOU MUST HELP ME, COL. MACAULAY.

BE CALM! IF YOU HAVE A PLAN, TELL ME ABOUT IT.

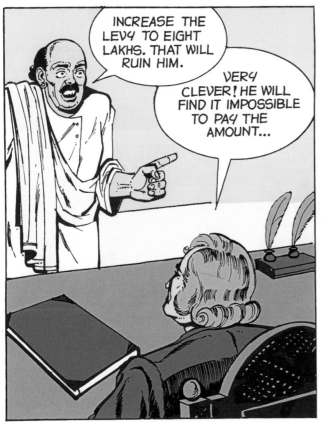

AT THE COURT OF THE MAHARAJA —

THE BRITISH ARE NOW DEMANDING EIGHT LAKHS OF RUPEES. THIS IS IMPOSSIBLE!

YOUR HIGHNESS, WE HAVE NO CHOICE. OUR REFUSAL TO PAY WILL ANTAGONIZE THE BRITISH.

WE CAN'T AFFORD TO DO THAT NOW. LET US SIGN THE TREATY AND THEN BIDE OUR TIME.

ALL RIGHT, THAMPI.

VELU THAMPI WAS FACED WITH THE DIFFICULT TASK OF RAISING EIGHT LAKHS OF RUPEES.

PADMANABHAN, I HAVE TO RAISE THE MONEY SOMEHOW. STERN MEASURES MUST BE TAKEN.

DO AS YOU THINK FIT, BROTHER.

HE INTRODUCED STERN MEASURES AGAINST HOARDERS...

VELU THAMPI IS STERN BUT JUST.

PEOPLE WILL THINK TWICE BEFORE HOARDING GOODS NOW.

...AND DISCIPLINE IN THE ARMY WAS TIGHTENED.

LAND REVENUE WAS REVISED ACCORDING TO THE YIELD OF THE LAND.

YOU ARE WELCOME, FOR I KNOW VELU THAMPI IS JUST AND FAIR.

WE ARE CONDUCTING A SURVEY TO ASSESS THE YIELD FROM YOUR LAND.

WHEN VELU WENT TO HIS ANCESTRAL HOME FOR A SHORT REST —

AH! HOW FORTUNATE I AM TO HAVE SUCH FERTILE FIELDS OF PADDY!

THE COCONUT CROP, TOO, IS VERY GOOD, MY SON.

MOTHER, IN WHAT CATEGORY DID THE OFFICIAL PLACE OUR FIELDS?

WELL, THEY SHOULD BE IN THE FIRST CATEGORY SEEING THAT THEY ARE SO FERTILE...

...BUT, AS A FAVOUR, HE PUT THEM IN THE THIRD. SO WE HAVE TO PAY LESS BY WAY OF TAX.

MOTHER, YOU SHOULD HAVE SET A GOOD EXAMPLE BY PAY- ING WHAT IS DUE FROM YOU.

WHAT YOU DID WAS WRONG...

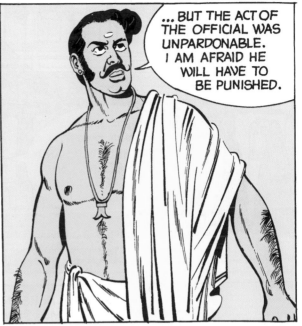

...BUT THE ACT OF THE OFFICIAL WAS UNPARDONABLE. I AM AFRAID HE WILL HAVE TO BE PUNISHED.

ON HIS RETURN TO TRIVANDRUM, VELU THAMPI SUMMONED ALL THE OFFICIALS.

LET IT BE KNOWN THAT HENCEFORTH CORRUPTION WILL NOT BE TOLERATED. NO MAN, RICH OR POOR, IS ABOVE THE LAW. THE LAW APPLIES TO EVERYONE EQUALLY—MYSELF INCLUDED!

MEANWHILE, BAD NEWS HAD REACHED TARAKAN.

MASTER, THE DIWAN HAS CONFISCATED ALL YOUR LAND BECAUSE YOU HAVE FAILED TO PAY YOUR TAXES.

OH, NO! I MUST GO AND SEE THE RESIDENT AT ONCE!

ONCE AGAIN, I COME TO YOU FOR HELP. MY LAND HAS BEEN CONFISCATED. I AM RUINED!

I SHALL PERSONALLY SEND A MESSENGER TO VELU THAMPI, ASKING HIM TO SPARE YOU.

VELU THAMPI REPLIED CURTLY, REFUSING THE RESIDENT'S REQUEST—

FOR YEARS, TARAKAN HAS OPPRESSED THE PEOPLE. NOW HE MUST PAY THE PRICE.

VELU THAMPI DARES TO REFUSE MY REQUEST? I'LL CRUSH HIM! I'LL ASK THE MAHARAJA TO DISMISS HIM.

WHEN THE MAHARAJA RECEIVED THE RESIDENT'S MESSAGE —

GO AND TELL THE RESIDENT THAT HE CANNOT GIVE ME ORDERS. I SHALL NOT DISMISS MY DIWAN.

VELU THAMPI WAS FURIOUS WHEN HE HEARD OF THE INCIDENT.

YOUR HIGHNESS, THE BRITISH CAN'T INTERFERE IN OUR DOMESTIC AFFAIRS. THE TREATY GIVES THEM NO SUCH RIGHTS.

THE BRITISH ARE MERE MERCHANTS. LET THEM STICK TO THEIR TRADING.

MACAULAY SEETHED WITH FURY AT THE ATTITUDE OF THE MAHARAJA.

SO HE REFUSES TO COMPLY? VERY WELL, INFORM HIS HIGHNESS THAT THE EIGHT LAKHS OF RUPEES HE OWES US MUST BE PAID NOW!

DISTANT FORTRESSES WERE REINFORCED...

... AND TROOPS WERE MOVED TO STRATEGIC POINTS.

THE TROOPS WERE KEPT IN FIGHTING TRIM.

THE MAHARAJA OF COCHIN HAS PROMISED TO SUPPORT US AGAINST THE BRITISH.

WE HAVE TO STAND TOGETHER IF WE ARE TO DEFEAT THE BRITISH.

THE FORCES OF VELU THAMPI CLASHED WITH THE BRITISH.

TOO LONG HAVE THE BRITISH OPPRESSED US. NOW WE SHALL BE FREE.

ON THE 18 TH OF DECEMBER, 1808 —

ONWARD, MY MEN! WE ARE AT THE GATES OF THE RESIDENCY!

THE RESIDENCY HAS FALLEN!

DOWN WITH THE BRITISH!

MACAULAY, HOWEVER, ESCAPED —

HE HAS ESCAPED! BUT DO NOT FEAR! WE SHALL CATCH UP WITH HIM.

BUT VELU THAMPI'S VICTORY WAS SHORT-LIVED.

THE BRITISH ARE GETTING FRESH TROOPS FROM MADRAS. WHAT SHALL WE DO?

COURAGE, BROTHER. WE WILL GET REINFORCE-MENTS FROM COCHIN.

DAYS PASSED, BATTLES WERE LOST, BUT —

THE REINFORCE-MENTS HAVE NOT YET COME.

OH, GOD! ARE WE TO BE DEFEATED AFTER TASTING VICTORY?

THE MIGHTY BRITISH NAVY BLASTED THE MAHARAJA'S FLEET.

YET VELU THAMPI REMAINED UNDAUNTED.

ONE LAST EFFORT, MY FRIENDS, AND WE SHALL SHAKE OFF THEIR YOKE — AND BE FREE.

THE PEOPLE WERE MOVED BY HIS IMPASSIONED PLEA FOR FREEDOM.

FREEDOM!

VELU THAMPI WILL LEAD US TO FREEDOM!

WE WILL DIE RATHER THAN BOW TO THE BRITISH!

BUT, ALAS! ONE BY ONE, THE TOWNS FELL TO THE BRITISH...

...AND FINALLY THEY CAME VERY NEAR TRIVANDRUM.

THE BRITISH ARE COMING!

ALL IS LOST!

TRIVANDRUM WILL FALL TO THE BRITISH ANY MOMENT NOW!

BROTHER, I HAVE ONE TASK LEFT....

VELU THAMPI HASTENED TO KILIMANOOR WHERE THE MAHARAJA WAS IN RESIDENCE.

I HAVE COME TO SEE HIS HIGH-NESS ON URGENT BUSINESS!

HERE I HAVE CONFESSED THAT I ALONE AM RESPONSIBLE FOR THE REBELLION AGAINST THE BRITISH AND THAT YOUR HIGHNESS AND THE PEOPLE KNEW NOTHING ABOUT MY PLAN.

IN THIS WAY, I SHALL SAVE MY RULER AND MY COUNTRY FROM THE WRATH OF THE BRITISH.

HERE IS MY SWORD, MY MOST CHERISHED POSSESSION. I HAND IT OVER TO YOU, MY SOVEREIGN, AND PLEDGE UNDYING LOYALTY.

VELU THAMPI!

YOUR HIGHNESS!

VELU THAMPI TOOK HIS FINAL LEAVE OF THE MAHARAJA —

WHAT WILL BECOME OF HIM NOW?

YOUR HIGHNESS, THE BRITISH HAVE TAKEN THE CAPITAL!

THERE IS NO POINT IN CONTINUING THIS UNEVEN BATTLE. TELL THEM I AM WILLING TO COME TO TERMS.

AND SO THE WAR ENDED.

WHAT A SAD END TO A VALIANT STRUGGLE!

WHAT WILL BECOME OF THE DIWAN NOW?

THE BRITISH TOOK OVER. THANKS TO VELU THAMPI'S NOBLE GESTURE, THE MAHARAJA CAME TO NO HARM. BUT HE WAS HELPLESS IN THE HANDS OF THE BRITISH.

THE BRITISH ARE DETERMINED TO HAVE THEIR REVENGE.

YOU ARE TO ARREST THE TRAITOR VELU THAMPI, AND EXECUTE HIM!
— BY ORDER OF THE RESIDENT

HOW CAN I ORDER THE ARREST AND THE EXECUTION OF MY FAITHFUL DIWAN?

BUT THE MAHARAJA HAD NO CHOICE.

GO AND FIND VELU THAMPI, WHEREVER HE MAY BE.

YES, YOUR HIGHNESS!

THE SEARCH FOR VELU THAMPI WAS ON —

BUT VELU THAMPI, THE BRAVE DIWAN, HAD GONE INTO HIDING, ALONG WITH HIS BROTHER.

COME QUICKLY, BROTHER, WE HAVE VERY LITTLE TIME.

THEY REACHED A DESERTED TEMPLE AT MANNADI.

WE SHOULD BE SAFE HERE.

THEY WILL NOT THINK OF SEARCHING THE TEMPLE.

THEY APPROACHED GODDESS BHAGAWATI—

WE HAVE MERELY GAINED A LITTLE MORE TIME, PADMANABHAN.

PROTECT US, O MOTHER!

I ONCE HAD A DREAM... THAT WE COULD SHAKE OFF THE YOKE OF BRITISH TYRANNY.

TODAY THAT DREAM LIES SHATTERED. BUT THERE WILL BE OTHERS TO CONTINUE THE STRUGGLE...

...AND EVENTUALLY, THE BRITISH WILL BE DRIVEN AWAY.

MEANWHILE THE BRITISH WERE INFORMED OF VELU THAMPI'S HIDE-OUT. THE NET CLOSED IN —

27

28

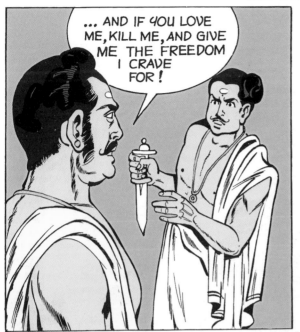

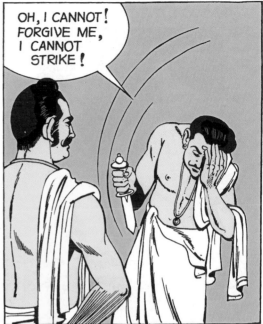

VERY SOON, THE TEMPLE WAS SURROUNDED BY THE BRITISH.

AT LAST! VELU THAMPI IS IN OUR HANDS!

THE SOLDIERS WERE TOO LATE. VELU THAMPI HAD ESCAPED.

YOU ARE TOO LATE! LOOK, THERE LIES VELU THAMPI! HE IS OUT OF YOUR REACH NOW!

SO HE'S DEAD ALREADY? NEVER MIND, WE'LL HANG HIS BODY UP— AND WE'LL HANG YOU TOO, FOR THAT MATTER!

BUT THE MEMORY OF VELU THAMPI, ONE OF THE FIRST OF OUR FREEDOM-FIGHTERS, LIVES ON.

TRAVANCORE

TRAVANCORE WAS A FORMER KINGDOM IN SOUTH INDIA. IT COVERED SOUTH KERALA, THE KANYAKUMARI DISTRICT AND THE SOUTHERNMOST TIP OF TAMIL NADU. IT WAS NOTED FOR ITS RELIGIOUS TOLERANCE. HINDUS, MUSLIMS, CHRISTIANS AND JEWS LIVED TOGETHER WITHOUT ANY CONFLICT.

THE RELIGIOUS HARMONY WAS SO STRONG THAT EVEN DURING THE TRAVANCORE-DUTCH WAR OF 1741, THE CHRISTIANS IN TRAVANCORE SUPPORTED THEIR HINDU KINGS OVER THE CHRISTIAN INVADERS.

TRAVANCORE WAS THE FIRST PRINCELY STATE TO ALLOW THE SO-CALLED 'LOWER' CASTES OF THAT TIME TO ENTER THE TEMPLES. WOMEN WERE GIVEN A LOT MORE FREEDOM IN TRAVANCORE THAN IN OTHER PARTS OF INDIA, OR EVEN THE WORLD. THEY WERE GIVEN THE FREEDOM TO DIVORCE AND MARRY AT THEIR WILL. THEY ALSO INHERITED PROPERTY AFTER THEIR PARENTS' DEATH, UNLIKE OTHER AREAS WHERE ONLY MEN INHERITED THE PROPERTY.

VELU THAMPI'S LEGACY

THE INDIAN GOVERNMENT HAS ISSUED A STATE STAMP IN VELU THAMPI'S HONOUR. THE GOVERNMENT OF KERALA HAS CREATED A MEMORIAL TO THE GREAT HERO AT MANNADI, WHERE HE SPENT HIS LAST DAYS. THERE IS ALSO A STATUE OF HIM IN FRONT OF THE OLD SECRETARIAT IN THIRUVANANTHAPURAM.

VELU THAMPI'S SWORD REMAINED IN THE ROYAL FAMILY FOR OVER 150 YEARS. IN 1957 IT WAS GIVEN TO THE THEN PRESIDENT OF INDIA, RAJENDRA PRASAD. THE FAMOUS SWORD, WHICH WAS USED TO FIGHT THE BRITISH, IS NOW KEPT IN THE NAPIER MUSEUM IN THIRUVANANTHAPURAM.

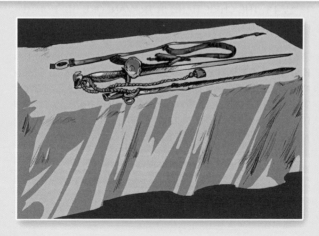

KUNWAR SINGH

HIS AGE WAS NO BAR TO HIS PASSION FOR FREEDOM

The route to your roots

KUNWAR SINGH

Kunwar Singh was seventy-five when he chose to fight the British. His story is part of the chain of events that surround the First War of Indian Independence. Even though he was on good terms with the British commissioner of Patna, Kunwar Singh was clear that his loyalties lay with the mutinying sepoys. He and his band of men caused enough disruption to have the British baying for his arrest. Sasaram, Rewa, Ramgarh, Atraulia – he seemed to be everywhere at the same time. And they never got him.

Script	Illustrations	Editor
Rajendra Sanjay And Appaswami	Souren Roy	Anant Pai

Cover illustration by: C.M. Vitankar

KUNWAR SINGH

BANG!

1857: A FOREST IN JAGDISHPUR, BIHAR —

SHABASH, BABU!

I CANNOT BELIEVE YOU ARE SEVENTY-FIVE!

MR. TAYLER, I HATE MYSELF EVERY TIME I SHOOT A TIGER.

I HAVE BEEN USING THIS RIFLE ONLY TO KILL POOR ANIMALS...

...AND NEVER IN A BATTLE.

YOU MUST THANK US FOR THAT, BABU.

1

YES, BABU KUNWAR SINGH. THAT'S WHAT THE BRITISH EMPIRE HAS ACHIEVED IN INDIA. NO MORE WARS BETWEEN PETTY PRINCIPALITIES.

THERE IS ONE STRONG CENTRAL AUTHORITY—THE AUTHORITY OF THE EAST INDIA COMPANY.

AND THOSE WHO NEED EXCITEMENT CAN ALWAYS SHOOT TIGERS!

OF COURSE, NOT!

DON'T TELL ME YOU WANT TO SHOOT ME INSTEAD! HA! HA!

YOU ARE A FINE GENTLEMAN, MR. TAYLER, YOU TRY TO UNDERSTAND US. WE HAVE GREAT RESPECT FOR YOU.

THE FEELING IS MUTUAL, KUNWAR SINGH.

I THANK YOU, MY FRIEND, FOR EVERYTHING.

YOU CONSIDER COMMISSIONER TAYLER A FRIEND, DON'T YOU?

IF YOU MEAN MR. TAYLER, THE MAN—**YES**.

IF YOU MEAN MR. TAYLER, THE COMMISSIONER OF PATNA—**NO**.

IS MR. TAYLER AWARE OF THIS?

WON'T IT COME AS A SHOCK TO HIM WHEN HE FINDS YOU ON THE SIDE OF THE REBELLIOUS SEPOYS?

THAT CAN'T BE HELPED.

BROTHER, YOU KNOW VERY WELL THAT THE REBELS STAND NO CHANCE OF SUCCEEDING. THEY WILL BE CRUSHED.

YOU COULD BE RIGHT, AMAR.

THEN WHY...?

I WILL TELL YOU WHY.

OUR SEPOYS ARE OPPRESSED. OUR COUNTRYMEN ARE OPPRESSED. OUR PLACE IS WITH THEM, NOT WITH THE OPPRESSORS.

JUNE 1857: PATNA —

NO, MY DEAR MAN. I DON'T AGREE WITH YOU. KUNWAR SINGH IS ABSOLUTELY RELIABLE.

MR. TAYLER, TEN YEARS AGO SOMEONE THREW A PARCEL INTO A WELL IN PATNA.

WE RETRIEVED THE PARCEL.

IT CONTAINED LETTERS TO LEADERS IN PATNA INVITING THEM TO RISE AGAINST THE GOVERNMENT.

AND THE LETTERS BORE THE DISTINCT IMPRESSION OF KUNWAR SINGH'S SEAL!

BUT HE WAS NOT ARRESTED BECAUSE THE PROOF WAS NOT CONCLUSIVE.

I BEG YOUR PARDON, SIR. IT WAS NOT FOR WANT OF PROOF. WE WERE AFRAID THAT HIS ARREST WOULD MAKE PEOPLE ANGRY...

IT IS FOR THE SAME REASON THAT I DON'T WANT TO LAY MY HANDS ON KUNWAR SINGH NOW.

I AM MORE WORRIED ABOUT THE SEPOYS AT DINAPORE.

DELHI HAS FALLEN. CAWNPORE HAS FALLEN. AGRA IS IN PERIL. AND BEFORE THE SEPOYS AT DINAPORE RISE...

... WE MUST DISARM THEM.

JULY 24, 1857: DINAPORE —

CAPTAIN DUNBAR, DISARM THE NATIVE SEPOYS. TAKE BACK THE PERCUSSION CAPS* ISSUED TO THEM.

YES, GENERAL LLOYD.

WE HAVE THE TROOPS OF THE THIRTY-SEVENTH FOOT AS A STANDBY, IN CASE...

LET'S HOPE THERE WON'T BE ANY TROUBLE.

AT THE SPECIAL AFTERNOON PARADE —

...SO WE WANT YOU TO GIVE UP THE PERCUSSION CAPS ISSUED TO YOU...

YOU WANT THE CAPS, DO YOU? HERE, TAKE THEM.

BANG!

THE BRITISH SOLDIERS PANICKED AND RETURNED FIRE.

BANG!

FIRE!

* SMALL QUANTITIES OF GUNPOWDER, WRAPPED IN PAPER ETC. USED AS A DETONATOR

6

JULY 26, 1857: ARRAH, THE HEADQUARTERS OF SHAHABAD DISTRICT —

THIS, MR. WAKE, WILL BE OUR FORTRESS TILL HELP ARRIVES. IT'S THE BEST I COULD DO.

I HAD THESE SANDBAGS PILED UP HERE. WE COULD OPEN FIRE FROM BEHIND THEM.

WHAT ABOUT THE BUILDING OPPOSITE?

I GOT THE WALL AROUND THE ROOF KNOCKED DOWN THERE.

SO THAT ANYONE WHO COMES FROM THAT DIRECTION WILL BE EXPOSED TO OUR FIRE.

GOOD WORK, MR. BOYLE. LET'S GO IN.

OH, MR. WAKE! I'M SO FRIGHTENED.

THERE'S NO NEED TO PANIC, MY DEAR. WE HAVE FIFTY SIKHS AND TWELVE ENGLISH-MEN TO DEFEND US...

...TILL HELP ARRIVES FROM PATNA.

WHERE ARE THE MUTINEERS, MR. WAKE?

BANG!

THERE! YOUR QUESTION HAS BEEN ANSWERED.

OUTSIDE THE FORTIFIED HOUSE—

THE WHOLE TOWN IS TAKEN RAJA SAHEB, EXCEPT FOR THIS HOUSE.

LAY SIEGE TO THE HOUSE AND POST SCOUTS TO KEEP A LOOK-OUT. I AM SURE A RESCUE PARTY WILL SOON ARRIVE.

MEANWHILE, I'LL SEE THAT LAW AND ORDER IS MAINTAINED IN THE TOWN.

JULY 29, 1857 —

RAJA SAHEB, A BOAT-LOAD OF EUROPEANS AND SIKHS HAS BEEN SPOTTED WAY DOWN THE RIVER.

SO THEY HAVE ARRIVED AT LAST.

SHALL WE PREVENT THEM FROM LANDING?

NO. LET THEM LAND. LET THEM CROSS THE BRIDGE TOO. THEN...

AT THE BRIDGE —

CAPTAIN, SHALL WE REST OUR MEN FOR A WHILE WHEN WE'VE CROSSED THE BRIDGE?

NO! WE MARCH ON.

JULY 30, 1857 —

A FEW MORE MILES TO GO...

AH!

BANG!

MOST OF THE MEN IN THE RESCUE PARTY WERE KILLED IN THE AMBUSH. THE FEW WHO SURVIVED RAN FOR THEIR LIVES.

AUGUST 2, 1857 —

RAJA SAHEB, THE ENEMY HAS BEEN SIGHTED NEAR BIBIGANJ!

WE'LL MOVE ON THERE, THEN.

LATER, AT THE FORTIFIED HOUSE OF MR. BOYLE —

OUR TORMENTORS HAVE VANISHED.

WHAT COULD HAVE HAPPENED?

SOME TIME LATER —

OPEN THE DOOR!

AT LAST! OUR MEN!

I WOULD LIKE TO MEET MR. WAKE.

I AM MR. WAKE.

GOOD MORNING, SIR. I AM MAJOR VINCENT EYRE OF THE BENGAL ARTILLERY.

I WAS ON MY WAY TO ALLAHABAD WHEN I HEARD ABOUT THE SITUATION HERE. I TOOK THE ROAD TO ARRAH.

I MUST THANK PROVIDENCE FOR SENDING YOU THIS WAY.

ANOTHER DAY AND WE WOULD HAVE SURRENDERED.

BY THE WAY, DID YOU SUFFER HEAVY CASUALTIES?

NOT REALLY. THE REBELS THREW UP THEIR ARMS SOONER THAN WE EXPECTED AND FLED TO JAGDISHPUR.

WE WILL MARCH ON TO JAGDISHPUR AS SOON AS REINFORCEMENTS REACH US.

I HAVE BEEN PLEADING WITH PATNA TO SEND TROOPS. BUT THERE HAS BEEN NO RESPONSE, MAJOR EYRE.

ANY EUROPEAN MOLESTED OR KILLED?

NO, SIR. NOT A SINGLE EUROPEAN WAS HARMED. THE MUTINEERS SHOWED THAT MUCH CONSIDERATION.

A FEW DAYS LATER—

I AM CAPTAIN RATTRAY OF THE SIKH REGIMENT, SIR.

AT LAST PATNA HAS WOKEN UP!

MR. WAKE, IT IS DIFFICULT TO SPARE TROOPS. EUROPEANS ARE RUSHING FROM MUZAFFARPUR, GAYA AND CHAMPARAN TO PATNA FOR PROTECTION.

THE RAMGARH INFANTRY HAS REVOLTED. SO HAS THE HAZARI-BAGH INFANTRY. AND MR. TAYLER HAS BEEN REPLACED BY MR. SAMUELLS AS THE COMMISSIONER OF PATNA.

EACH ONE HAS HIS OWN PROBLEMS I GUESS.

LET US NOT WASTE ANY TIME. WE MUST CAPTURE KUNWAR SINGH BEFORE HE JOINS THE MUTINEERS FROM HAZARIBAGH.

HOWEVER, WHEN THEY BURST INTO KUNWAR SINGH'S RESIDENCE AT JAGDISHPUR—

THE BIRD HAS FLOWN!

CONFISCATE THE AMMUNITION! DESTROY WHAT WE CANNOT CARRY AND BLOW UP THE BUILDINGS!

LATER —

CAPTAIN, I CAN NOW RESUME MY JOURNEY TO ALLAHABAD.

I HOPE YOU SUCCEED IN CATCHING THAT WILY, OLD FOX. GOOD LUCK!

AT PATNA MESSAGES STARTED POURING IN.

KUNWAR SINGH WAS SEEN AT SASARAM.

KUNWAR SINGH HAS TAKEN REWA!

KUNWAR SINGH PASSED THROUGH RAMGARH!

THIS OLD MAN OF SEVENTY-FIVE IS LEADING US A PRETTY DANCE, I DARE SAY!

HERE IS THE LATEST MESSAGE, SIR.

HE JOINED HANDS WITH NANA SAHEB AND FOUGHT TO RECAPTURE CAWNPORE.* WE WON.

DID WE TAKE HIM CAPTIVE?

NO, SIR. AT THE MOMENT HE'S CAMPING AT ATRAULIA.

WE'RE LUCKY HE'S NOT FORTY YEARS YOUNGER!

* KANPUR

MEANWHILE, AT KOELSA* WHERE COLONEL MILMAN OF THE 37TH REGIMENT WAS CAMPING—

KUNWAR SINGH AND HIS MEN ARE AT ATRAULIA, COLONEL. HE'S CAMPING IN THE MANGO GROVE.

WE WILL STOP HIM BEFORE HE REACHES AZAMGARH.

COLONEL MILMAN MARCHED THROUGH THE NIGHT...

...AND REACHED ATRAULIA.

WE'RE JUST IN TIME.

IN THE PITCHED BATTLE FOUGHT IN THE MANGO GROVE...

...MILMAN SCORED AN EASY VICTORY.

THAT WAS A GOOD JOB WASN'T IT, COLONEL?

OUR MEN HAVE EARNED A REST. ARRANGE FOR BREAKFAST!

✳ NEAR AZAMGARH

15

BIHAR

Script: Swarn Khandpur.
Illustrated by: S.K. Parab

TOWARDS THE END OF THE TWELFTH CENTURY, MUHAMMAD-BIN BAKHTIYAR KHALJI INVADED NALANDA AND THE UNIVERSITY TOWN OF ODANTPURI (MODERN BIHAR-SHARIF). HE FOUND A LARGE NUMBER OF BOOKS THERE. ON BEING TOLD THAT THE TOWN WAS A VIHARA, A PLACE OF LEARNING, HE TOO CALLED IT VIHARA, WHICH BY AND BY, BECAME BIHAR.

BIHAR HAS BEEN DESCRIBED AS THE RICHEST STATE OF THE COUNTRY AS IT IS ABUNDANTLY ENDOWED WITH RICH MINERALS LIKE IRON AND COAL. TWO BIG STEEL PLANTS AND SEVERAL OTHER INDUSTRIES HAVE BEEN SET UP IN THE STATE.

THE MAHATMA GANDHI SETU OVER THE RIVER GANGA WHICH FLOWS RIGHT ACROSS BIHAR CUTTING IT IN TWO, IS THE LONGEST RIVER BRIDGE IN THE WORLD.

ONE OF THE WORLD'S BIGGEST CATTLE AND ELEPHANT FAIRS IS HELD AT SONPUR, ON THE RIVER GANDAK, NEAR PATNA. FOR A MONTH IN OCTOBER-NOVEMBER, THOUSANDS OF PEOPLE THRONG HERE COMBINING BUSINESS WITH PLEASURE.

PATNA, THE CAPITAL OF BIHAR WAS FOUNDED BY SHER SHAH SUR, AT THE SITE WHERE THE ANCIENT CITY OF PATALIPUTRA WAS. FROM A PETTY AFGHAN CHIEF...

...SHER SHAH ROSE TO BECOME THE 'EMPEROR OF HINDUSTAN'.

HIS TOMB AT SASARAM LIES IN SHAHABAD DISTRICT WHERE KUNWAR SINGH, THE BIHAR HERO OF 1857, ROSE AGAINST THE BRITISH.

ONE OF THE MOST FASCINATING PLACES IN PATNA IS THE KHUDA BAKSH ORIENTAL LIBRARY. IT CONTAINS SOME OF THE RAREST MANUSCRIPTS ON ISLAMIC LITERATURE, PRICELESS MINIATURES AND PAINTINGS.

SOON —

AH! TEA!

JUST THEN —

COLONEL! IT WAS ONLY THE VANGUARD THAT WE REPELLED. KUNWAR SINGH IS ADVANCING WITH THE BULK OF HIS ARMY.

WHAT!

WE'LL MEET HIM! COME ON, BOYS.

MILMAN'S EVERY MOVE WAS WATCHED BY KUNWAR SINGH'S MEN HIDING IN SUGAR-CANE FIELDS...

...BEHIND MUD WALLS...

...AND ATOP TREES.

18

FIRE!

MILMAN LOST HEAVILY.

WE'LL HAVE TO RETREAT!

KUNWAR SINGH'S MEN CHASED THEM RIGHT UP TO AZAMGARH.

HURRY! TO THE ENTRENCHMENT WITHIN THE JAIL.

KUNWAR SINGH'S MEN TOOK OVER THE TOWN AND THREW A BLOCKADE ROUND THE JAIL.

SEE THAT NO ONE ESCAPES.

HOWEVER, MESSENGERS HAD ALREADY LEFT WITH THE NEWS.

AT ALLAHABAD THE GOVERNOR-GENERAL, LORD CANNING CONFERRED WITH SENIOR OFFICERS.

KUNWAR SINGH'S PLAN IS TO DASH OFF TO BANARAS*!

IF HE TAKES BANARAS HE WILL EFFECTIVELY CUT US OFF FROM CALCUTTA ON THE ONE HAND AND ALLAHABAD AND LUCKNOW ON THE OTHER.

I AGREE WITH YOU, COLONEL MARK. YOU MUST PREVENT HIM FROM REACHING BANARAS.

I WISH YOU ALL THE BEST.

* VARANASI

MEANWHILE AT AZAMGARH —

OUR REPEATED EFFORTS TO TAKE THE JAIL HAVE MET WITH FAILURE, RAJA SAHEB.

THEN WE SHOULD MOVE ON TO BANARAS.

A FEW HUNDRED MEN ARE ENOUGH TO CONTINUE THE BLOCKADE OF THE JAIL.

I BEG TO DIFFER, SIR.

WE SHOULD TAKE AZAMGARH BEFORE WE MOVE ON.

OUR STRENGTH LIES IN MOBILITY. WE HAVE TO STRIKE HARD AND MOVE ON...

...BEFORE THE ENEMY RECOVERS AND HITS BACK.

WITH DUE RESPECT TO YOU RAJA SAHEB...

I THINK YOU ARE WRONG, IN THIS CASE.

THE ENTRENCHMENT WILL SOON FALL. IT'S ONLY A MATTER OF DAYS.

BATTLES ARE LOST IN A MATTER OF HOURS.

WE WISH TO STAY ON AT AZAMGARH AND...

ALL RIGHT. BUT...

...I KNOW IT IS NOT THE RIGHT DECISION.

I ONLY PRAY I AM PROVED WRONG.

UNFORTUNATELY KUNWAR SINGH WAS PROVED RIGHT. COLONEL MARK MANAGED TO REACH AZAMGARH WITH THE SPEED OF LIGHTNING.

HE FOUGHT HIS WAY THROUGH THE BESIEGERS...

...AND JOINED THE MEN INSIDE THE ENTRENCHMENT.

BUT WORSE WAS TO FOLLOW.

RAJA SAHEB, A WHOLE INFANTRY BRIGADE IS ON ITS WAY.

WHAT DO YOU SUGGEST? SHOULD WE FIGHT?

WE WILL BE BUTCHERED, RAJA SAHEB.

LUGGARD IS LEADING THE BRIGADE...

ALL RIGHT. WE WILL GO BACK TO ARRAH.

WHO WILL VOLUNTEER TO HOLD LUGGARD'S MEN AT BAY WHILE THE REST GET AWAY?

I WILL, RAJA SAHEB, WITH MY MEN.

IT WAS NISHAN SINGH, KUNWAR SINGH'S TRUSTED GENERAL.

THUS WHEN SIR LUGGARD, THE VETERAN BRITISH COMMANDER, REACHED THE RIVER TONS, HIS MEN WERE GREETED BY A VOLLEY OF BULLETS.

MEANWHILE, KUNWAR SINGH GOT AWAY WITH THE MAIN ARMY.

A COUPLE OF DAYS LATER, NISHAN SINGH JOINED KUNWAR SINGH.

LUGGARD HAS ANNOUNCED AN AWARD OF 25,000 RUPEES FOR YOUR HEAD, RAJA SAHEB.

AT LAST THE BRITISH HAVE RECOGNISED THE WORTH OF INDIANS!

AND THE MAN WHO WANTS TO CLAIM THE REWARD IS BRIGADIER DOUGLAS!

GOOD LUCK TO HIM.

AT NIGHT —

DOUGLAS HAS CAUGHT UP WITH US, RAJA SAHEB.

I WANT YOU TO GET AWAY WITH THE MAIN ARMY.

DIVIDE YOUR MEN INTO TWO GROUPS. EACH GROUP SHOULD TAKE A DIFFERENT ROUTE AND MEET AT A CONVENIENT PLACE LATER.

KUNWAR SINGH HELD THE ENEMY AT BAY...

...LONG ENOUGH TO ENABLE THE MAIN ARMY TO GET AWAY. THEN HE ALSO JOINED NISHAN SINGH. TOWARDS EVENING —

SHALL WE REST OUR MEN FOR THE NIGHT?

LEAVE SUCH LUXURIES TO DOUGLAS. WE MUST MARCH ON.

KUNWAR SINGH'S MEN MARCHED DAY AND NIGHT...

...TILL THEY REACHED MANIAR.

WELCOME, RAJA SAHEB.

AT LAST WE ARE AMONG FRIENDS.

KUNWAR SINGH'S MEN RESTED AT MANIAR.

RAJA SAHEB, MAY I ASK YOU A QUESTION... IF YOU DON'T MIND?

GO AHEAD.

ARE WE GOING TO WIN THIS WAR?

IF YOU WANT AN HONEST ANSWER...

... NO. WE WILL NOT WIN THIS WAR.

THEN WHY WAR AT ALL? IT DOESN'T MAKE SENSE. I MEAN ...

DO YOU REMEMBER TIPU SULTAN ... AND HOLKAR?

OF COURSE, I DO, RAJA SAHEB. WHO CAN FORGET THEM?

WHEN TIPU FELL IN DISTANT MYSORE I WAS A LITTLE BOY IN BIHAR.

NOW AT THE AGE OF SEVENTY-FIVE, I STILL REMEMBER WHAT PEOPLE SAID ABOUT HIS WAR...

... THE WAR HE LOST... THE WAR THE BRITISH WON.

WHO IS THIS LITTLE BOY?

MY GRANDSON.

WE WILL LOSE THIS WAR. BUT YOUR GRANDSON AND A THOUSAND OTHERS WILL CONTINUE THE FIGHT.

AND GOD WILLING, THEY WILL WIN.

MEANWHILE AT THE BRITISH CAMP —

WE HAVE POSITIVE INFORMATION THAT KUNWAR SINGH IS GOING TO CROSS THE GANGES...

AT WHICH SPOT?

WE'LL GET THAT INFORMATION SOON, BRIGADIER. HE HAS NO BOATS.

HE WILL HAVE TO USE ELEPHANTS TO CROSS THE RIVER.

GOOD. THAT GIVES US AN ADVANTAGE OVER HIM.

AT MANIAR —

THE ENEMY HAS SWALLOWED THE STORY FED TO THEM.

GOOD!

27

THAT NIGHT AT SHEOPUR GHAT —

THE BOATS ARE READY, RAJA SAHEB.

LET THE MEN CROSS OVER.

I WILL STAND GUARD.

WHILE KUNWAR SINGH'S MEN WERE ROWING AWAY ...

...DOUGLAS' MEN WERE LOOKING FOR ELEPHANTS!

NO SIGN OF THEM HERE.

I THINK WE HAVE BEEN TAKEN FOR A RIDE.

BY THE TIME THE TIRED MEN ARRIVED AT THE RIGHT PLACE, KUNWAR SINGH'S MEN HAD CROSSED THE RIVER, ALL EXCEPT TWO HUNDRED.

LOOK!

FIRE!

KUNWAR SINGH WAS BOARDING THE LAST BOAT WHEN A BULLET HIT HIM IN THE LEFT WRIST.

HE UNSHEATHED HIS SWORD...

...CUT OFF THE INJURED WRIST...

...AND RESUMED HIS JOURNEY.

APRIL 23, 1858: KUNWAR SINGH WAS BACK IN HIS OWN VILLAGE.

BRIGADIER DOUGLAS TOO HAD CROSSED THE GANGA AND WAS CAMPING AT ARRAH.

I NEED MORE MEN TO TAKE ON THE OLD WARRIOR ON HIS HOME GROUND.

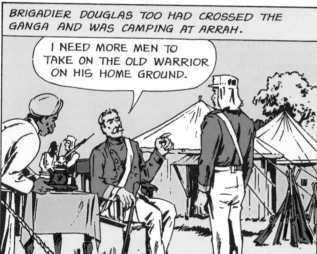

LET'S AWAIT THE ARRIVAL OF SIR LUGGARD.

LITTLE DID DOUGLAS KNOW THAT AT THAT VERY MOMENT THE OLD LION WAS ON HIS DEATHBED, WITH AMAR SINGH BY HIS SIDE.

BROTHER, I PROMISE I WILL CONTINUE THE FIGHT.

KUNWAR SINGH SMILED...

...AND CLOSED HIS EYES NEVER TO OPEN THEM AGAIN.

A COLLECTOR'S EDITION,
FROM INDIA'S FAVOURITE STORYTELLER.

India's greatest epic, told over 1,300 beautifully illustrated pages.
The Mahabharata Collector's Edition. It's not just a set of books, it's a piece of culture.

THE MAHABHARATA
COLLECTOR'S EDITION
Rupees Two thousand, four hundred and ninety-nine only.

2I Inspiring
Stories of Courage

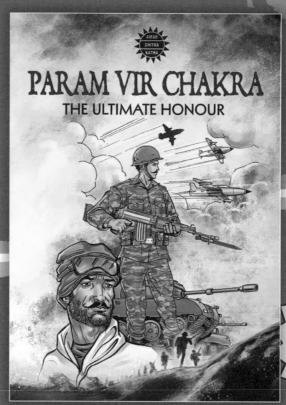

PARAM VIR CHAKRA
THE ULTIMATE HONOUR

To buy this product, visit your nearest bookstore
or buy online at **www.amarchitrakatha.com** or call: **022-49188881/2/3/4**